THE MOVIE BUFF'S BOOK

THE MOVIE BUFF'S BOOK

Edited by
TED SENNETT

Pyramid Books　　　　　　**New York**

Layout and Design by ANTHONY BASILE

ACKNOWLEDGMENTS

I should like to thank all the writers who contributed to this book for their expertise and their cooperation. And a very special thanks to Curtis Brown, who checked all the quizzes with his usual patience, diligence, and vast knowledge.

As always, my deepest thanks go to my family and especially my wife Roxane, who endured yet another book with good grace and humor.

Photographs: Jerry Vermilye, The Memory Shop, Gene Andrewski, Cinemabilia, United Press International, Walt Disney Productions, Culver Pictures, Museum of Modern Art Stills Collection, Academy of Motion Picture Arts and Sciences, and Columbia Pictures.

CONTENTS

Introduction, by Ted Sennett 9

ONE: FAMILIAR FACES 11

   That Hamilton Woman, by Jerry Vermilye 12
   The Meanest Man in the Movies, by Gary Collins 18
   Who's That Again? 24
   Family Albums—Hollywood Style 25
   The Movie Connection 26
   Unfinished Business 27
   The Name Game 38
   The Versatile Players 39
   The Golden Silence 40
   Professionally Speaking 41
   They Had Character 42

Movie Matters: Random items on movies and movie people 51

TWO: ALL ABOUT FILMS 55

   Forgotten Movies, by Howard Thompson 56
   Songs, Dances, and Snappy Sayings 62
   The Ills That Flesh Is Heir To 65
   "And I Quote . . ." 66
   The Movie Scene 68
   Do It Again 77
   The Barroom Brawl: Notes on Visual Clichés in the Movies, by Robert F. Moss 78
   Foreign Matter 83
   To the Ladies 84
   Gentlemen of the Movies 85

Murder and Mayhem 86
Phantoms of the Movies, by Curtis F. Brown 88
Disney and His Friends 90
Them Thar Hills 92
Rule, Britannia! 94
A Crossword Puzzle for Movie Buffs, by Curtis F. Brown 96

More Movie Matters: Gleanings From the Silent Era 97

THREE: THE MOVIE THEATRE—FROM PALACE TO "NABE" 103

Where Fantasy Reigned: The Glorious Roxy Theatre, by Ted Sennett 104
Saturday Marathon at the Movies, by William Wolf 110
The Golden Movie Palaces of Hollywood, by Foster Hirsch 115
The "Nabes," by Ted Sennett 120

Still More Movie Matters 124

FOUR: THE PEOPLE BEHIND THE CAMERA 131

"Now You See It, Now You Don't": The Art of Movie Magic, by René Jordan 132
Gentleman Raoul, by Jeanine Basinger 143
The Director's Chair (I) 150
The Director's Chair (II) 151
The Movie Songsmiths 153
Unheralded and Unsung 154
James Wong Howe, by Nicholas Yanni 157
Gregory La Cava, by Stephen Harvey 162
Quiet on the Set 171

Answers to Quizzes 184
About the Contributors 192

INTRODUCTION

By Ted Sennett

How would you define a movie buff?

As with the blind men describing an elephant, your definition depends on where you stand at the moment. Some buffs are intense but happy creatures who thrive in darkness, ferreting out facts about performers like Douglas Fowley, Almira Sessions and Rondo Hatton. Others prefer to watch a Ukrainian drama on alienation, a French farce on sexual identity, or a three-hour allegory on the Vietnam War, made with a hand-held camera. Still others lean to "auteurist" explanations of films by Nicholas Ray, Don Siegel or Jerry Lewis. And many movie buffs, of course, have the capacity to embrace Carmen Miranda as well as Luis Buñuel, to enjoy the Three Stooges as much as Fellini's clowns, to delight in a Pete Smith short or an Andy Warhol marathon.

Generally, however, a movie buff is a person who loves films, who takes pleasure in being amused, moved, frightened, or enlightened by them—a person who views film as an art and a diversion, sometimes simultaneously.

This book has been created for movie buffs of every kind. Its goal is to entertain, inform, and challenge movie fans with a variety of materials: articles on all aspects of film by writers who share my life-long devotion to movies; quizzes designed to test even the longest movie memories; photographs of favorite players and films, including many never published before, and scores of facts about movies even self-proclaimed "experts" may not know.

We movie buffs are a hardy breed, often braving inclement weather and enduring out-of-focus projection, uncomfortable seats and noisy audiences to watch an admired film or performer. But when we watch with lovers' eyes, all defects, all difficulties tend to fade.

And that, after all, may be the simplest and best definition of a movie buff I can offer.

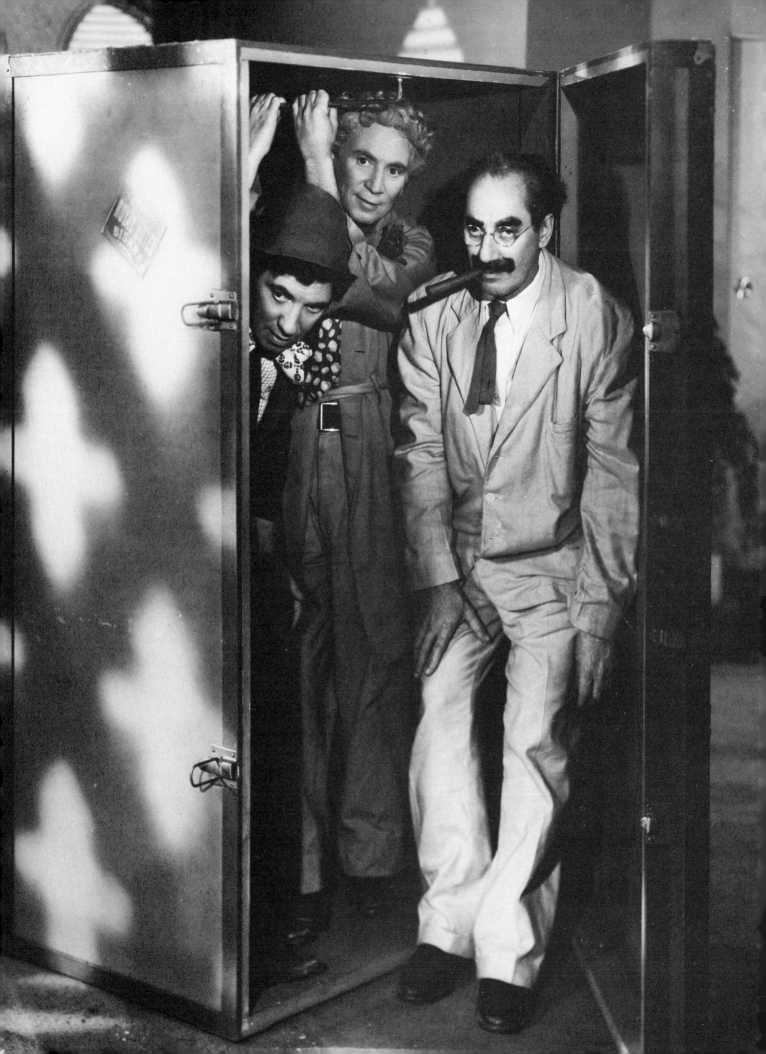

ONE:
FAMILIAR FACES

In this first section, we have brought together articles and quizzes about the players whose faces, personalities, and skill at keeping audiences riveted in their seats are an integral part of movie magic. These include the charismatic stars, of course, but also those gifted and durable supporting players for whom every movie buff feels deep affection and gratitude for a lifetime of memories.

We begin with an article on one of my personal favorites: the screen's most lovable hatchet-faced crone, Margaret Hamilton. . . .

THAT HAMILTON WOMAN

By Jerry Vermilye

Mention Margaret Hamilton to the average person and you may get a blank stare. Identify her as the Wicked Witch of the West in *The Wizard of Oz*, and you're likely to get an immediate sound of recognition—and appreciation.

Not many still-active performers of advanced years can claim that they're best known for a performance they gave thirty-six years ago and, in this case, the actress' perpetuity can be credited to television, where that 1939 movie classic is kept alive in annual reprises. Each year audiences can renew their pleasure in the magic blend of ingredients that have conspired to keep the late Judy Garland forever young and innocent, "Over the Rainbow" a forever-popular tune—and Margaret Hamilton forever America's favorite witch.

Filmed during the winter of 1938–39, this retelling of L. Frank Baum's well-loved children's story gave no indication during production of the perennial classic it was destined to become. The story had been filmed twice during the silent era—in long-forgotten 1910 and 1925 versions, neither of which *had* a wicked witch!

Billed seventh in a cast that featured, in support of Judy Garland, the likes of Frank Morgan, Ray Bolger, Bert Lahr, Jack Haley and Billie Burke, Margaret Hamilton almost didn't get the dual role of the Wicked Witch and Miss Elmira Gulch, the hatchet-faced, vindictive, bike-riding Kansas neighbor who tries to have Dorothy's little dog, Toto, killed. According to Hamilton, Gale Sondergaard gave her strong competition for the part, and perhaps the reason that she finally won it was due as much to Sondergaard's vanity (she was determined that she'd be a *beautiful* witch) as to Hamilton's favorable test (for which she was encouraged to express her own conception of the character in wardrobe and makeup). Though she knew and loved Baum's famed Oz books, the actress held out little hope that she'd get the role. "You want something," she recalls, "and someone else gets it, and you learn to be philosophical about it." Then, while attending a football game with friends, she met the film's producer, Mervyn LeRoy, who asked her whether she'd like to play the part. She and her agent requested a guarantee of ten weeks' employment, and got fifteen. Before shooting was completed, she had worked for twenty-three weeks.

Margaret Hamilton seldom has anything bad to say

about anybody, and she holds fond memories of Judy Garland and the rest of her *Wizard of Oz* co-workers. With the aid of MGM's special-effects wizard Arnold Gillespie, Hamilton's green-complected Wicked Witch was made to seem fully capable of whizzing around the skies on her broomstick, casting flaming missiles at her enemies, and appearing and disappearing in great explosions of fire and smoke. During one such vanishing act, the actress was seriously burned when a flash-pot, planted inside the trap door which enabled her to vanish before the smoke cleared, ignited her costume.

Nor was the rest of filming *The Wizard of Oz* all fun and games. She recalls, "I would imagine that no one in that cast ever worked that hard again. Each day seemed harder than the one before, but we all cared so much about the film that we tried not to let our fatigue show through. The worst for me was the makeup for the witch. It was deathly hot under the lights, and I couldn't go too long without nearly perspiring it all off. Ray Bolger,

13 GHOSTS (1960)

Bert Lahr and Jack Haley all had the same kind of problems. The one who kept us all going was Judy Garland. Her freshness and vitality is something I will never forget. And wonderful Victor Fleming, the director, worked harder than any man I have ever seen to make that film the best of its kind that had ever been done. I don't think Hollywood will ever top it."

But aside from the physical strain of playing her celebrated part, Hamilton modestly minimizes her contribution. "It's not my idea of the greatest piece of acting. It's not a particularly difficult role. A witch is a witch. There's not much you can do to make it different. Anyone can play a witch. All you do is roll your hands, cry in a shrilly manner, and rant and rave. It's not very hard."

"*The Wizard of Oz* keeps coming back every year," says the actress, "because it's such a beautiful film. I don't think any of us knew how lovely it was at first. But after a while, we all began to feel it coming together—and we knew we had something."

Years later, Margaret Hamilton re-created her *Wizard of Oz* witch in a musical stage adaptation that played such far-flung summer theatres as Brunswick, Maine and Dallas, Texas. In her only other contribution to theatrical black magic, she has appeared onstage as the First Witch in at least two different productions of Shakespeare's *Macbeth*.

When not playing witches, Margaret Hamilton has enjoyed a long and respectable career of enacting the sort of characters she does best—waspish busybodies, folksy neighbors, and gossipy maids and housekeepers, often disapproving of others. Sometimes, however, the characters she plays are as kindly and considerate as the real-life woman, an actress well loved by those fortunate enough to have worked with her in films, stage or television for nearly half a century, from supporting roles in regional theatre at the Cleveland Play House to stardom in her later years. In the 1974 touring edition of Stephen Sondheim's charming hit musical, *A Little Night Music*, taking on the grande-dame role created by Hermione Gingold, she shared billing with Jean Simmons.

The Wizard of Oz hardly marked the beginning of Margaret Hamilton's movie career. By then, she had already appeared in some twenty-five films, starting in 1933 with MGM's *Another Language*, in which she was among the few chosen to repeat the roles they had created in the original stage version of Rose Franken's successful play. Here she was an all-wise daughter-in-law, munching grapes as she commented humorously on the events in this comedy-drama about the problems of a mother-dominated family. Her success in this film won her a contract with RKO, where she first brought her unique comedic talents to the brief role of Madame DuBarry, a flashily frocked milliner who trades quips with prosecutor Ricardo Cortez in the courtroom melodramatics of *Hat,*

THE WIZARD OF OZ (1939). With Clara Blandick, Judy Garland, and Charley Grapewin

Coat and Glove (1934).

In the 1935 Fox remake of D. W. Griffith's 1920 melodrama *Way Down East,* after long specializing in roles requiring mostly well-intentioned wit or homespun humor, Margaret Hamilton first turned mean on the screen as Martha Perkins, the venomous New England country gossip whom *The New York Times'* critic André Sennwald found "vastly amusing." The following year, in *These Three*, William Wyler's first film version of Lillian Hellman's controversial play *The Children's Hour,* she left the malevolence to young Bonita Granville, brilliantly cast in the pivotal role of schoolgirl Mary Tilford, whose vindictive lies destroy several adult lives. Hamilton was a perceptive servant employed by this little monster's grandmother and in one scene she was required to slap the youngster. The actress recalls that Bonita repeatedly pleaded, "Don't hit me hard—please don't hit me hard." Margaret Hamilton reports, "We did it about five times and each time I let myself pull back a lot when I hit her. Finally Mr. Wyler said, 'Come on now, do it right and get it over with.' I hauled back and cracked her one, and you could hear the report of it around the set, and the imprint of my hand was left on poor Bonita's face. It really was hard for me to do; I loved Bonita dearly."

Close on the heels of *These Three* was Hamilton's comic gem of a New England boardinghouse keeper in the amusing Paramount comedy, *The Moon's Our Home* (1936). Blunt and businesslike, she's at her best in the hilarious scene in which she secretly models Margaret Sullavan's flimsy nightgown before her bedroom mirror, only to be discovered by her flabbergasted hayseed husband, Spencer Charters.

Among Margaret Hamilton's memorable character parts in movies, one recalls the W. C. Fields-Mae West

13

THE WIZARD OF OZ (1939). With Judy Garland and Ray Bolger

comedy-Western, *My Little Chickadee* (1940), in which she helped garner the film's sporadic laughs as Mrs. Gideon, the self-righteous town gossip who sets out to see the ill-reputed Flower Belle Lee (West) redeemed by an honest man—one who'll *marry* her. Hamilton's scenes weren't many, but who can forget the one on the train in which she shares a seat—and a brief flirtation—with Cuthbert J. Twillie (Fields), whose obvious preoccupation with the adjacent Flower Belle upsets Mrs. Gideon to the point where Fields comments, in an aside to the audience, "I hope she doesn't get too violent. I don't have the strength to knock her off the train." Filming this sequence, Margaret Hamilton remembers, Fields got a bit carried away, continuing to ad-lib and improvise with her long after the script's pages were completed. So fascinated was she by the occasion that she gladly went right along with the gag, even after the cameras stopped shooting. Of her seven weeks of work on this comedy, she says, "I never laughed so much in my life."

One day on the Universal lot where *My Little Chickadee* was being filmed, Hamilton took advantage of a lull in shooting to approach Mae West to confirm the rumor that West had *requested* her for the part of Mrs. Gideon. Acknowledging that she had indeed asked producer

Lester Cowan to give her the role, West added in that inimitable, insinuating voice, "I *like* your *work*!"

Although she became aware of animosity between West and Fields on the set, Hamilton personally had no problems with either of them. "I loved Mr. Fields," she says. "He was really a fine person. He never used bad language or told off-color stories if there were women present. You know how show people are, and if they got into an off-color-joke session on that set and women were there, he would walk away. He was always respectful and polite to women. He was a gentleman in the old-fashioned—and every sense—of that word."

Hamilton credits Fields' own self-indulgence with causing friction with Mae West. "Like every comedian I have ever known, he fell in love with his own performance and repeated it endlessly. Miss West would let him go on for a while, but finally she'd say, 'All right, Bill, that's enough of that! Shall we settle down and get on with the job?' And that hurt his feelings."

In 1941, Margaret Hamilton ably supported a declining John Barrymore (as a nutty professor-inventor) in the wacky shenanigans of *The Invisible Woman,* in which she played his faithful housekeeper. Despite the derogatory tales she had heard about Barrymore, she recalls,

14

"He was, I can say, a thorough professional, on his best conduct, and completely considerate." And she adds, "A lot has been made of the fact that he sometimes read his lines from prompt boards, but he made those lines so meaningful, so fully understood his role and the parts of the other performers, and was so dedicated to doing an honest day's work that he impressed us all."

She also has the highest regard for James Cagney, with whom she worked in *Johnny Come Lately* (1943), a sentimental costume drama about an enterprising fellow who helps an old lady (Grace George) save her failing newspaper. Of him she says, "He was a painstaking actor, rehearsed in great detail, and was always interesting to watch and work with."

One movie that Hamilton recalls with particular pleasure is Preston Sturges' *The Sin of Harold Diddlebock* (or *Mad Wednesday*, as it was later retitled), a film largely unfamiliar to current audiences and, for some reason, unavailable to television. Filmed all during 1945 and well into 1946, this slapstick "comeback vehicle" for comedian Harold Lloyd cost some two million dollars, an exorbitant sum for a mid-1940s black-and-white farce. Made under the aegis of the eccentric and wealthy Howard Hughes, it had a limited distribution in 1947 under its lengthy original title, but was withdrawn from release when neither critics nor public responded with much enthusiasm. Hughes later released a trimmed and re-edited version in 1950 as *Mad Wednesday*—to little effect.

Margaret Hamilton holds pleasant memories of this film. "They had limitless money, and they used to take us to long lunches every day at a very expensive restaurant which, of course, was very enjoyable and made for good will."

Cast as Harold Lloyd's spinster sister, she sported horn-rimmed glasses similar to those which were Lloyd's trademark. "I was a little bit of a battle-ax," she recalls, describing her big scene—one in which a hung-over Lloyd comes home late, after an alcoholic binge, to face his sister, who clamps his ten-gallon hat on her own head and delivers a tirade. She remembers, "It was one very long sentence with at least six possible hysterically funny climactic pauses, and at rehearsal I played it for each laugh." But Preston Sturges instructed her to try the whole sentence without a pause, sacrificing a few laughs for the one big one at the end. "I guarantee it will be the biggest in the picture," he promised her. And she acknowledges that it was.

About the film's star, Margaret Hamilton says, "Mr. Lloyd, just like W. C. Fields, never knew when to stop. When he created a comic effect, he went on and on. In the film he went into a bank with a huge lion on a leash. But then he took that pet and roamed in and

THESE THREE (1936). With Bonita Granville

THE INVISIBLE WOMAN (1941). With John Barrymore

THE SIN OF HAROLD DIDDLEBOCK (1947) (re-issued in 1950 as MAD WEDNESDAY). With Harold Lloyd

out of so many banks that it wasn't funny any longer. Unfortunately, Mr. Hughes and Mr. Sturges had a falling out, and Mr. Sturges was not allowed to cut his own picture. Whoever did it let Harold Lloyd go on and on, and I can't help feeling that this caused at least part of the failure."

Margaret Hamilton was at her most rambunctious in 1950's *Wabash Avenue,* a Betty Grable period musical in which the actress played temperance leader Tillie Hutch, a militant battle-ax who wreaks havoc in Phil Harris' saloon. She calls it, "the best fight I ever had."

With her hawklike nose, shrewd, fish-eyed glances and firmly clamped, decisive mouth, Margaret Hamilton, even as a young actress, was shuttled into character parts, often playing older women. Consequently, among her early stage roles in Cleveland were such classic spinsters as Miss Prism in Wilde's *The Importance of Being Earnest* and Prossy in Shaw's *Candida.* In her twenties, Margaret Hamilton trained as a kindergarten teacher, a career which she pursued for a number of

years, both in New York City and her native Cleveland, where she was born on December 9, 1902, the fourth and youngest child of an attorney and his organist wife.

Thanks to television commercials, Margaret Hamilton has become anonymously familiar to a large segment of the public, who might not realize that the gentle-voiced Emily Tipp, the cartooned Tip-Top Bread lady, or Cora, that nice, folksy promoter of Maxwell House Coffee (the *only* coffee she claims to sell at her old New England country store) is the same actress they once loved to hate in *The Wizard of Oz.* But commercials (and their subsequent residuals) have kept the actress solvent when film roles were few (recent appearances have included brief, amusing turns in 1970's *Brewster McCloud* and 1971's *The Anderson Tapes*), and have enabled her to travel about the country, performing in plays and musicals that seldom pay the kind of wages earned by an actor in movies and television.

Though that unusual face has long been Margaret Hamilton's fortune, it has also limited her to eccentric roles for which most producers have been prone to typecast her. However, in summer and regional theatre productions, she has occasionally enjoyed variations in casting that have proven her adept at sophisticated comedy or down-to-earth drama. These roles have included Mrs. Fisher, the testy mother in George Kelly's *The Show-Off*, Mrs. Dudgeon (one of her favorite parts) in Shaw's *The Devil's Disciple,* and Julia, the wise and witty friend-of-the-family (a role eliminated from the film version) in Samuel Taylor's *Sabrina Fair*. That she has, for some time, performed in stage musicals like *Oklahoma!, Showboat, Goldilocks* and now *A Little Night Music*, indicates the extent of the talents of this indefatigable, multimedia lady. (She won nightly spontaneous applause simply by kicking up her heels during a dance number in the unsuccessful 1969 Ray Bolger musical, *Come Summer*.)

Late in 1972, while in Hollywood for a cameo role as a crusty professor in the ABC-TV movie *The Night Strangler,* Margaret Hamilton talked about the kind of acting challenges that still interest her. "I'd never been asked to play this kind of intellectual woman before, and I found it a little tricky," she said. "The language was the most difficult I have ever encountered because the words were all scientific. I'm thankful that the director, Dan Curtis, was so patient with me. He had a lot to put up with."

At seventy-two, retirement doesn't seem to interest Margaret Hamilton, although she admits, "I find I don't have to work as much any more to stay happy. My career has been good to me, and I enjoy coming out to Hollywood to do a part, if it's something new. Otherwise, I'm content just to stay at home and relax with other things I love to do." (Divorced for many years, the actress has a married son and grandchildren who occupy her leisure interests, when she isn't busy with what used to be called "good works.")

And once each year, she's still the all-time super-witch to millions of American television viewers as *The Wizard of Oz* again allows Margaret Hamilton to screech, rant, brew evil potions, menace Judy Garland and finally—doused by a fatal bucket of water—dissolve quickly away with that memorable, anguished cry, "I'm melting!" And melt away she does, though we know she'll be back to amuse, frighten and entertain us all over again.

BREWSTER McCLOUD (1970)

THE MEANEST MAN IN THE MOVIES

By Gary Collins

Over the years movie villains, like movie heroes, have come in a remarkable variety of shapes and sizes. Unlike the heroes, however, they have enjoyed a distinct advantage in commanding our attention and interest. Whereas the actions of the hero are governed by a fairly rigid standard of conduct, the villain has been limited only by the range of his own resourcefulness. Whether motivated by the prospect of ill-gotten gains, unlimited power, revenge, or the simple joy of perpetrating a misdeed, the genuinely inspired bad guy, like any creative spirit, earns the admiration of everyone who appreciates a sense of dedicated professionalism. The more dedicated the villain, in fact, the greater his claim to lasting fame, a rule which has found probably its strongest support in the career of the late Bela Lugosi, the most consistently cunning, diabolical, and ruthless of all movie villains.

To the vast majority of moviegoers, Lugosi has always been identified with his performance in *Dracula* (1931), the Tod Browning version of Bram Stoker's famous novel. The longevity of the association has been due, no doubt, to the fact that Lugosi's portrayal of the infamous count was indeed the result of fortuitous casting. So totally did he represent what everyone expected the ultimate vampire would be like, that his performance became the yardstick by which all later interpretations were measured. Succeeding Draculas may

have been more "modern" in concept, or even closer to the Stoker original, but none could really match Lugosi in that suggestion of sheer menace and total evil which gave the character its grip on the popular imagination. What is surprising, then, in view of the extent to which he made the part his, is the fact that Lugosi played the role only once after his original appearance, and then not until seventeen years later in *Abbott and Costello Meet Frankenstein* (1948). Throughout his entire career, in fact, Lugosi's genuine vampire roles were extremely few, with his appearance as Armand Tesla in the underrated *Return of the Vampire* (1943) being the only one on a par with Dracula.

What rivaled the number of real vampires in Lugosi's films were the simulated ones, where his masquerades were obviously designed to capitalize on the interrelationship between Lugosi the man and Lugosi the vampire in the public mind. Cast as the vaudevillian who poses as Count Mora in order to assist Lionel Barrymore in solving a murder case in *Mark of the Vampire* (1935), Lugosi was in a sense already playing "himself" a mere four years after *Dracula* had made his name a household word. In time, the boundary between fantasy and reality was blurred even further, with the result that characters, and even entire films, could be built around Lugosi's personality. As Nardo the magician in *Spooks Run Wild* (1941), he looked suspiciously like the Dracula

DRACULA (1931). With Helen Chandler

of old with his black cloak and coffins, and this link with a reality outside the film led Leo Gorcey, Huntz Hall and the East Side Kids to suspect him of a recent series of vampire-like murders. In *The Corpse Vanishes* (1942), he slept in a coffin for no apparent reason but that it pleased him, while in *Vampire Over London* (1952) he was a madman who *thought* he was a vampire. Finally, in *The Boys From Brooklyn* (1953) also known significantly as *Bela Lugosi Meets a Brooklyn Gorilla*, the duality of his existence was acknowledged within the film itself by comedian Sammy Petrillo's specific references to Lugosi's vampire past. *Dracula,* then, did more than simply elevate Lugosi to a well-deserved stardom. On the one hand, it did typecast him, but at the same time it also added resonance to many of his later roles, giving them a larger-than-life quality which was very much in keeping with the basic spirit of the films themselves.

This is not to suggest, of course, that Lugosi could never vary his own impact on a movie audience, or submerge himself in the demands of a character part. He was remarkably effective as the half-human Sayer of the Law in *Island of Lost Souls* (1933), where he functioned as the hirsute spokesman for the bizarre "manimals" who owed their semihuman existence to Charles Laughton's skill in speeding up the evolutionary process. In tones both supplicating and indignant, Lugosi led this grotesque band in chanting the various precepts of the Law, each one of them concluding with the haunting and rhetorical "Are we not men?" Few roles ever allowed Lugosi to make such effective use of his magnificent voice, and even his villainous potential was given its full head when he led his surging cohorts in vivisecting Laughton for the fadeout.

No less inspired were his appearances as Ygor, the shaggy-haired, broken-necked shepherd who greatly enhanced the appeal of two of Universal's entries in the long-running Frankenstein saga. Hell-bent on a somewhat justified quest for revenge, he spent the better part of *Son of Frankenstein* (1939) using the Monster to destroy the self-righteous jurors who had sentenced him to the gallows for grave robbing. Supposedly killed by Basil Rathbone, he turned up again in *The Ghost of Frankenstein* (1942), and managed to convince mad scientist Lionel Atwill that Ygor's brain in the Monster's body would make for a unique combination of intelligence and strength. "I have the strength of a hundred men! I cannot die! I cannot be destroyed! I, Ygor, will live forever!," he shouted in exhilaration following the operation, moments before he went blind because of a slight miscalculation concerning blood types. Nevertheless Ygor's brain was now the Monster's, and thus it

WHITE ZOMBIE (1932)

MURDERS IN THE RUE MORGUE (1932). With Arlene Francis

seemed bizarrely appropriate that Lugosi himself was cast as the Monster in the next entry in the series, *Frankenstein Meets the Wolf Man* (1943). The result, however, was disastrous, with Lugosi weighted down by a makeup job that neither concealed his own distinctive features nor managed to create any semblance of what the famous creature was supposed to look like.

What Lugosi did have that could not be duplicated was the singular appeal of his face and voice. Even on those rare occasions when he was somewhat less than a total villain, or when he functioned primarily as a red herring, Lugosi's demeanor suggested undertones of malevolence, whether they were present in the character or not. Boris Karloff was the real villain in *The Black Cat* (1934), but as a Hungarian psychiatrist bent on revenge against him, Lugosi was sufficiently ambiguous in his intentions to wind up being shot by David Manners. He was little more than an unconscious tool of his murderous wife in *The Invisible Ghost* (1941), but his pointed conversation with an empty chair at the very beginning of the film was certainly not designed to reassure any casual observer.

More important, then, than Lugosi's acting ability, or lack of it, was the undeniable force of his simple presence on the screen, which, supported by studio publicity, made him into perhaps the only great movie villain whose existence as a villain seemed so tangible and consistent.

Lugosi did not become different characters so much as it appeared that the camera merely intruded itself periodically into his affairs, leaving the audience to conclude that he would continue on exactly the same course once it left. Nowhere was this truer than in roles which Lugosi essayed most often, as the maddest of mad doctors and a master criminal the likes of which have rarely been seen since the end of his tenure. So inextricably interwoven was the image of the real Lugosi—the limited movie star whose erratic career constantly alternated between the heights and the depths—with the image of the perpetually thwarted mad scientist and master criminal, that these roles transformed him into an object of cult worship.

Functioning somehow like oblique references to his real life, these roles allowed Lugosi the exaggerated expression of hopes and frustrations which almost certainly had their counterparts in reality. How appropriate, for example, that the man who never totally regained the position of prominence he enjoyed so briefly as Dracula, should seek, as Roxor in *Chandu the Magician* (1932), to acquire a death ray that would have the entire world "groveling" at his feet. However, twenty years later, when the prospect of world domination beckoned again, in *Vampire Over London,* it was a tired Lugosi who acknowledged that he was no longer up to the demands of such an effort. Regaling an assistant with his plans

20

MARK OF THE VAMPIRE (1935). With Carol Borland

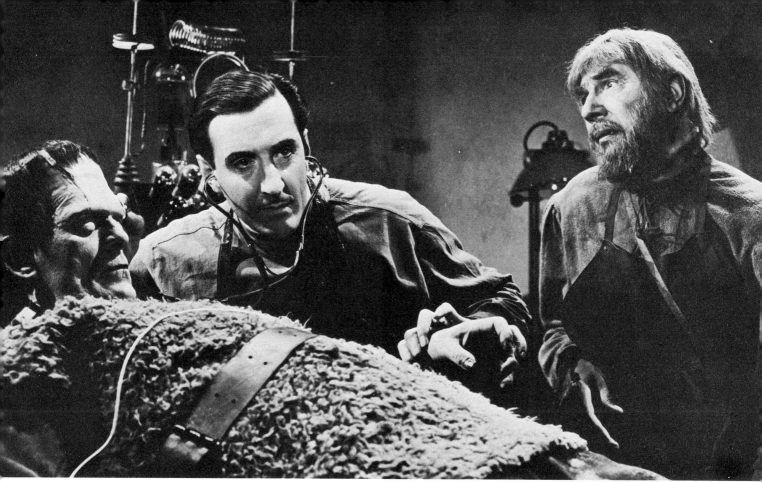

SON OF FRANKENSTEIN (1939). With Boris Karloff and Basil Rathbone

for building fifty thousand robots to help them in the endeavor, his answer to a question concerning how many have been built so far is a rather sheepish "Unnhh . . . err . . . one."

Lugosi's career may have fluctuated wildly over the years, but what never varied was the intensity of his own involvement. Just as he always gave of his best, even in the lowest of low-budget features, his mad doctors were totally dedicated to the project at hand, to the exclusion of all other considerations. Like Hawksian professionals gone mad, in fact, they could never find anyone who believed as strongly as they did in the pride that accompanied a job well done. "A true scientist is married to his profession," Lugosi tells John Carradine in *The Return of the Ape Man* (1944) when Carradine expresses a desire to abandon their ten-month Arctic search for the "missing link." And when an indignant Carradine points out later that a proposed brain transplant will leave the donor an idiot, Lugosi's response is characteristic: "And what about science?"

What never helped Lugosi's cause, of course, was the fact that his immediate goal, like his own stardom in the less-than-respected genre of the horror film, tended to be of questionable value to society at large. "I shall try to transplant a segment of the brain of a present-day man into the skull of that prehistoric creature, endowing him with just enough understanding to make him obey my orders," he says in a moment of inspiration which ultimately produced a confused creature who divided his time between committing murders and playing the "Moonlight Sonata" on a piano. "My life is consecrated to *great* experiment!" he intoned in *Murders in the Rue Morgue* (1932), as he attempted to prove the Darwinian theory of evolution by combining the blood of his pet ape, Erik, with that of various young girls. For sheer hard work, however, Lugosi reached what had to be his peak in *Bowery at Midnight* (1942) where, as a psychology professor doing research for a new book, he operated a Bowery mission as a front for his underworld activities, hoping to gain firsthand knowledge of the workings of the criminal mind.

Because of their questionable validity, such endeavors never attracted the best and the brightest in the way of assistants, with the result that Lugosi was afflicted with an endless procession of bunglers and malcontents who were forever thwarting his well-laid plans. Admittedly, working for Lugosi was not an easy task, and his authoritarian measures earned him a well-deserved reputation as the strictest of disciplinarians. When one of his minions in *Chandu the Magician* endured great hardship simply to report back to him on the failure of a particular operation, his reward was to have the man's eyes burned out with hot pokers. By the time of *Bowery at Midnight*, the rate of attrition in the ranks had risen to the point where Lugosi was forced to maintain his own private graveyard in order to accommodate those who had either been given to momentary lapses of loyalty or had simply outlived their usefulness.

Compounding this sticky labor-management problem was Lugosi's ill-disguised contempt and lack of consideration for both the abilities, however meager, and well-being of his subordinates. "Yes, once he was a great doctor. Now he's just a human derelict," he says of an old wino who was one of his crew in *Bowery at Midnight*. Not surprisingly, it is that same human derelict who does him in at the conclusion. When Lugosi's single-mindedness results in the deaths of his two chief assistants in *The Corpse Vanishes,* it remains for their crone of a mother to firmly implant a knife between his shoulder blades as he prepares to make his getaway. But it was *Ghosts on the Loose* (1943) which had the distinction of providing the ultimate summation of

Lugosi's relationship with his subordinates. "Is this some *more* of your bungling, you stupid fool?" he asks the latest in a long line of incompetents, and then, almost as though addressing an unpitying God, "*Why* do I have such idiots around me?"

Well might he ask, for it always seemed that no matter how carefully laid his plans, inexorable Fate had foredoomed Lugosi to failure because of a weak link somewhere in the chain, some fatal flaw either in himself or in his organization which he was never quite successful in overcoming. Nevertheless, our hope for his possible success is never completely dampened, and it is that faint flicker which keeps our eyes glued to the screen, nursing the belief that in spite of everything this *could* be the one occasion when Lugosi will surmount the obstacles placed in his path by a merciless Fate. The fact that he never does matters not at all, for the joy derives from his attempts rather than their results, and his unflinching fidelity to the highest standards of movie villainy reaffirms once more the maxim that true glory indeed lies not in winning or losing, but in how one plays the game.

GHOST OF FRANKENSTEIN (1942). With Evelyn Ankers and Lon Chaney, Jr.

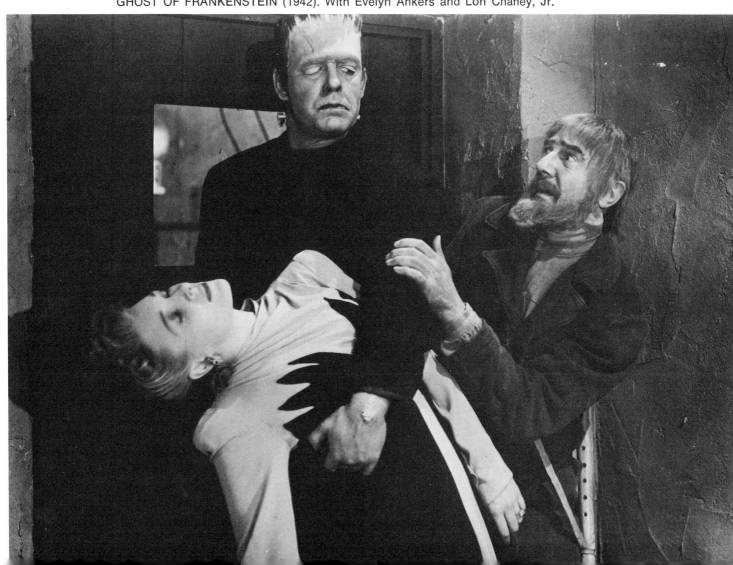

WHO'S THAT AGAIN?

The careers of many film stars often extend over so many years that it is sometimes difficult to recall when they were first making their mark in motion pictures. It is edifying to read the very first critical remarks on the durable performers.

In each instance below, we are quoting from the reviews received by a film star in *The New York Times* in his or her first major role or first English-language role. Can you identify the star and the movie?

1. "Although she is not precisely a newcomer to films, _____ is a slender, elfin and wistful beauty, alternately regal and childlike in her profound appreciation of newly-found simple pleasures and love."

2. "_____, in his film debut, is the bright particular star of this occasion. As the virtuous farm boy he plays with an immensely winning simplicity which will quickly make him one of our most attractive screen actors."

3. "Plainly a girl with whom to cope, slumberous of eye and softly reedy along the lines of Veronica Lake, she acts in the quiet way of catnip and sings a song from deep down in her throat."

4. "_____, fourteen-year-old soprano, carols most sweetly in an immature, but surprisingly well-trained voice. Her notes are rounded, velvety and bell-like; the manner of her rendition is agreeably artless; she has, besides, an ingratiating impudence which peppers her performance and makes it mischievously natural."

5. "_____, who has a dancer's talents, has been pressed a bit too far in his first film role. He has been forced to act brassy like Pal Joey during the early part of the film, and then turn about and play a modest imitation of Sergeant York at the end. The transition is both written and played badly."

6. "She wears the costumes of yesteryear with much grace and her fascinating delivery of English is apt to remind the onlooker of Marlene Dietrich's speech in Hollywood films."

7. "As the most startling innovation in way of a screen character in years—a fascinating fatalist, reckless and poor and unhappy, who smokes too much, who is insufferably rude to everybody, and who assumes as a matter of course that all the cards are stacked against him, _____ is such a sweet relief from conventional screen types, in this one character, anyway, so eloquent of a certain dispossessed class of people, that we can't thank Warner Brothers, Michael Curtiz, the director, Mr. Epstein and Miss Coffee, the screen playwrights, and even Miss Fannie Hurst, the original author, enough for him."

8. "The dancing of _____ and Miss Crawford is most graceful and charming. The photographic effects of these scenes are an impressive achievement."

9. " 'His voice,' says Mr. Iturbi, 'has quality and warmth and he has a very nice personality.' Check. We'll wait to see how he can act. A slight disposition to be too radiant and follow Mickey Rooney's footwork style betrays his youthful inexperience. No doubt, he will improve."

10. "_____, a recruit from Broadway and video, who is making his film debut in the role of Basil, bears a striking resemblance to Marlon Brando, but his contribution is hardly outstanding. As a youth who has been cheated of his rich inheritance by a covetous male, sold into slavery and eventually chosen to create the Holy relic, he is given mainly to thoughtful posing and automatic speech-making."

11. "_____, as the veteran who endures the most difficult time, is so vividly real, dynamic and sensitive that his illusion is complete. His face, the whole rhythm of his body and especially the strange timbre of his voice, often broken and plaintive and boyish, are articulate in every way."

12. "This young actor, who is here doing his first big screen stint, is a mass of histrionic gingerbread. He scuffs his feet, he whirls, he pouts, he sputters, he leans against walls, he rolls his eyes, he swallows his words, he ambles slack-kneed—all like Marlon Brando used to do. Never have we seen a performer so clearly follow another's style."

13. "_____ sings charmingly. In fact, the microphone takes to her singing better than to her speaking, and as she was there last night and said a few words to the spectators, it was quite evident that the fault lay with the microphone and not with Miss _____'s voice."

14. "_____, who was seen in Kenyon Nicholson's play, *The Barker*, lends her charm to this obstreperous piece of work. She seems quite at home before the camera."

15. "London's favorite American actress, _____, made her talking film debut last night. . . . At moments she is not unlike Marlene Dietrich and she has the same deep voice. She is mistress of her many scenes, whether they are where she is living in luxurious surroundings, enjoying an evening in a cabaret, or serving as a saleswoman in a dressmaker's establishment."

(*Answers on page 184*)

FAMILY ALBUMS—
HOLLYWOOD STYLE

Often over the years, Hollywood has seen fit to cast its fictional families with performers who seem to bear no actual resemblance to each other. Below is a list of such unlikely relatives. In each case, name the film in which they were related. (Score four points for each correct answer. Any score over 80 indicates that you know your Hollywood families.)

1. Myrna Loy as Shirley Temple's sister
2. Robert Young as Norma Shearer's son
3. Billie Burke as Joan Crawford's mother
4. Martha Raye as W. C. Fields' daughter
5. Dean Martin as Wendy Hiller's brother
6. Edmund Gwenn as Katharine Hepburn's father (No extra points, but an appreciative pat on the head if you can name *two* films in which they were father and daughter)
7. Robert Wagner as Spencer Tracy's brother

8. Greta Garbo as Scotty Beckett's mother
9. Ruth Hussey as Jerry Lewis' mother
10. Mickey Rooney as Jean Harlow's brother
11. Claude Rains as Dick Powell's brother
12. Wallace Beery as Jane Powell's father
13. Danielle Darrieux as Jane Powell's mother
14. Dan Dailey as Margaret Sullavan's brother
15. Maria Ouspenskaya as Robert Cummings' grandmother
16. Elvis Presley as Angela Lansbury's son

17. Johnnie Ray as Ethel Merman's son
18. Lee J. Cobb as Yul Brynner's father
19. Robert Taylor as Alla Nazimova's son
20. Marjorie Main as Humphrey Bogart's mother

21. Jane Wyman as Dame Sybil Thorndike's daughter
22. Don Ameche as Eugenie Leontovich's son
23. Frank Sinatra as Molly Picon's son
24. Jackie Cooper as Lana Turner's brother
25. Sophie Tucker as Judy Garland's mother

(*Answers on page 184*)

THE MOVIE CONNECTION

In each case, indicate the movie (as opposed to personal) connection between the performers cited i. e., they played the same role, or type of role, or they were associated on film with the same actor or actress. Score five points for each correct answer. A score of 80 or more demonstrates a well-honed movie mind at work.

1. Angela Lansbury and Jean Arthur
2. Mary Astor and Grace Kelly
3. Laird Cregar and Walter Huston
4. Veronica Lake and Kim Novak
5. Maurice Chevalier, Don Ameche, and Danny Kaye
6. Ginger Rogers and Jerry Lewis
7. Rex Harrison and Louis Jourdan
8. Leslie Howard and Laurence Harvey (two possible answers)
9. Dorothy McGuire and Jane Wyman
10. Kathryn Grayson and Eleanor Parker
11. Elisabeth Bergner, Tallulah Bankhead, and Bette Davis.
12. Herbert Marshall and Gladys Cooper*
13. Van Heflin and Charlton Heston
14. Betty Hutton and Barbara Stanwyck
15. Susan Kohner and Jeanne Crain
16. Greta Garbo and Jean Simmons
17. Siobhan McKenna and Dorothy McGuire
18. Alla Nazimova and Rita Hayworth
19. Jean Arthur and Doris Day
20. Fay Bainter, Fay Holden, Spring Byington and Ann Shoemaker

*a connection other than that they both appeared in the 1943 film, *Forever and a Day*

A bonus question for no points: What is the movie connection between Josephine Hutchinson and Nancy R. Pollock?

(Answers on page 184)

26

UNFINISHED BUSINESS

Not infrequently, a film production is begun and then quickly scuttled for one reason or another: an ill, irreplaceable, or inadequate star, a dwindling budget, or legal problems. Sometimes the film fragment is lost forever; sometimes it is absorbed into a new version, with new cast members and even a new director.

Here are a number of rare photographs taken from uncompleted productions.

In 1928, young Joan Crawford began a film called *Tide of Empire*. She was replaced by Renee Adoree whom, in turn, Crawford replaced in *Rose Marie*. Here is a scene from the uncompleted *Tide of Empire*.

Thirty-seven years after *Tide of Empire*, Joan Crawford was co-starred with Bette Davis in the Gothic melodrama, *Hush . . . Hush, Sweet Charlotte*. Illness forced her to retire from the role of Davis' vengeful cousin, and she was replaced by Olivia de Havilland.

In the original, uncompleted version of Kathleen Winsor's popular novel, *Forever Amber*, Peggy Cummins played the bed-hopping Amber. Here is the actress in full costume for the role. She was replaced by Linda Darnell in the 1947 movie.

Hedy Lamarr and Walter Pidgeon in a scene from the original, uncompleted version of *I Take This Woman* (1939), directed by Josef von Sternberg. A completely different version, directed by W. S. Van Dyke, was released in 1940. In this version, Kent Taylor replaced Walter Pidgeon.

The Painted Veil (1934). With Greta Garbo and Beulah Bondi. This scene was cut from the film and Miss Bondi was replaced by Bodil Rosing.

In 1937, Alexander Korda began *I, Claudius*, an ambitious film based on Robert Graves' novel about ancient Rome. Many problems, especially the injuries sustained by co-star Merle Oberon in a car accident, caused the production to be shut down before it was completed. (In 1965, a television film called *The Epic That Never Was* showed considerable footage from the aborted movie.) Here is Charles Laughton as the Emperor Claudius.

I, Claudius. Merle Oberon as Lavinia.

I, Claudius. With Emlyn Williams and Charles Laughton
(kneeling)

Often a scene is cut from the release print of a film, for any one of a number of reasons: it is considered extraneous or irrelevant; it impedes the action; it creates legal difficulties, or it simply makes a long film even longer.

Here are a number of photographs of scenes never viewed by audiences in the theatres:

In *Double Indemnity* (1944), Fred MacMurray was an insurance man trapped in an adulterous, murderous relationship with Barbara Stanwyck. In the end he is caught by insurance investigator Edward G. Robinson and sentenced to die in the gas chamber. In the release print of the film, the gas-chamber sequence was excised; here is a photograph from that sequence.

A "never-seen" scene from *Desire Me* (1947). Florence Bates, as an innkeeper named Joo-Lou, consoles widow Greer Garson. The scene did not appear in the released version. (Incidentally, both George Cukor and Mervyn LeRoy directed the film at different times but neither took credit, and no director was listed anywhere!)

The Snake Pit (1948) Olivia de Havilland and Celeste
Holm as inmates of an asylum. The scene was cut from
the film.

A scene from *The World of Suzie Wong* (1960), with
France Nuyen and William Holden, before Miss Nuyen
was replaced by Nancy Kwan.

A musical sequence cut from MGM's 1946 musical, *Till the Clouds Roll By*, loosely based on the life of Jerome Kern. Kathryn Grayson and Johnnie Johnston in a hardly credible set for Kern's *Music in the Air*.

Patricia Neal and Stephen Boyd in *The Third Secret* (1964). This scene and Miss Neal were cut from the film.

In *The Loved One* (1965), the bizarre comedy about the American way of death, Robert Morse had appeared in a sequence with Jayne Mansfield. The sequence was deleted from the released version.

A Miracle Can Happen (1948, later re-titled *On Our Merry Way*). John Qualen and Charles Laughton in a scene cut from this multi-star comedy.

In *The Beginning or the End* (1947), MGM's movie about the development of the atom bomb, Agnes Moorehead was cast as a scientist working on the bomb. Legal problems with the actual scientist she portrayed prompted MGM to cut her scenes from the film. Here she is with Robert O. Davis.

Notorious (1946). Cary Grant, Lenore Ulric, Ingrid Bergman, and Claude Rains. Miss Ulric never appeared in the final print of the film.

Juarez (1939). At dinner: Harry Davenport, Bette Davis, Montagu Love, and Brian Aherne. The scene was excised from the movie.

THE NAME GAME

Betty Grable was actually named Betty Grable. Ava Gardner was born Ava Gardner. And Humphrey Bogart's real name was Humphrey De Forest Bogart. But there are many stars whose actual names would look rather odd on a theatre marquee.

Below are the real names of twenty-five stars, accompanied in each case with one of their lesser-known movies. Can you identify the stars for four points each?

1. Constance Ockleman in *The Hour Before the Dawn* (1944)
2. Ernest Bickel in *Good Dame* (1934)
3. Gladys Georgianna Greene in *Public Hero Number One* (1935)
4. Rosetta Jacobs in *Francis Goes to the Races* (1951)
5. Sarah Jane Fulks in *Tugboat Annie Sails Again* (1940)
6. Marion Michael Morrison in *Somewhere in Sonora* (1933)
7. James Stewart in *Captain Boycott* (1947)
8. Ruby Stevens in *Shopworn* (1932)
9. Guenther Schneider in *John Meade's Woman* (1937)
10. William Henry Pratt in *The Ape* (1940)
11. Emma Matzo in *Desert Fury* (1947)
12. Spangler Arlington Brough in *Murder in the Fleet* (1935)
13. Lewis Delaney Offield in *Madison Square Garden* (1932)
14. Roy Scherer, Jr., in *The Fat Man* (1951)
15. Shirley Schrift in *Larceny* (1948)
16. Lucille Vasconcells Langhanke in *Trapped By Television* (1936)
17. Frances Gumm in *Pigskin Parade* (1936)
18. Emanuel Goldenberg in *Dark Hazard* (1934)
19. Lily Chauchoin in *Secrets of a Secretary* (1931)
20. Edythe Marrener in *$1,000 a Touchdown* (1939)
21. Mary Tomlinson in *Tish* (1942)
22. Tula Ellice Finklea in *Fiesta* (1947)
23. Bernard Schwartz in *City Across the River* (1947)
24. Reginald Truscott-Jones in *Next Time We Love* (1936)
25. Isaiah Leopold in *Son of Flubber* (1963)

(Answers on page 185)

THE VERSATILE PLAYERS

Over the years, many favorite performers have appeared in an astonishing variety of roles, demonstrating their skill and versatility. In each case, name the performer who played all the roles indicated, and then the films in which he or she appeared in those roles. (Score two points for each performer named, and one point for each film named. Any score of 75 or more indicates that you are well acquainted with the careers of some of the screen's best-known, most admired players.)

1. A fatally flirtatious ranch foreman's wife; a New England doctor's frightened daughter who becomes insane; a share-cropper's gallant, tireless wife; a social-climbing ex-racketeer's beloved Daisy; mother to the town's most beautiful girl.

2. A sensitive young composer with a blind brother; a reckless but talented drunkard on the Yorkshire moors; a long-awaited caller on a shy, crippled girl; a no-account man who brutally rapes his stepdaughter; a troubled Michigan doctor who commits suicide.

3. A banker fleeing from the police for embezzlement; a genial and bibulous Washington reporter; a pilot whose neck is fatally broken in a crash; a New Hampshire doctor whose daughter-in-law dies in childbirth; a grandiloquent pool-player who poses as the husband of an old derelict.

4. A slum prostitute whose ex-boyfriend is a killer; a spangled fancy-lady known as "Countess" in the wild West; the alcoholic mistress of a kingpin crook; ambitious mother of a tennis-playing daughter; the Jewish mother of an aspiring actress; nasty wife to an expatriate film director.

5. A rough-hewn sailor washed up out of the sea; the Catholic Dean of Lourdes who champions a visionary girl; a gentle rancher who loves a half-breed girl; a Nova Scotia fisherman with a deaf-mute daughter; a compassionate film producer.

6. A grotesque bride to an equally grotesque groom; a feebleminded woman with a homicidal sister; a crackpot painter; henpecking nurse to a barrister; an antic witch.

7. The soulful sweetheart of celebrated swordsman and lover Don Juan; a scatterbrained and often-married princess; the serene matriarch of a turn-of-the-century family; an aging prostitute who befriends a hunted man; a selfish, bigoted New England mother bent on destroying her son's marriage.

8. A young man determined to prove his executed father's innocence; an itinerant ranch hand with a dim-witted friend; a comically demented pianist; an amiable and eccentric auto mechanic; a famous war correspondent.

9. A madcap, penniless Russian impresario; a theatrical producer with a fondness for young actresses; a fight manager with fighter and mistress trouble; a husband and father recently released from a mental hospital; a political boss out to control a presidential candidate.

10. An Italian soldier captured in the Libyan desert; the proud "paisano" father of a war hero; a simple father to a gifted violinist; an Italian-American detective in the early 1900s; Chief Sitting Bull.

11. The neurotic, romantically frustrated aunt of a spoiled brat; a spiteful matron with a selfish wartime attitude; a shrill murderess who falls from an open window; wife to the *Cotton Blossom*'s captain; a giddy, much-married countess; a slatternly servant in a strange household.

12. A fire-breathing preacher, bent on saving a woman sinner; a prosperous industrialist with a frivolous wife; a devilish itinerant peddler in New England around 1840s; a troubled doctor in an occupied Norwegian town; a toothless varmint and gold prospector.

13. The Ambassador from Sylvania; Buffalo Bill; a disreputable and double-crossing lawyer; an Associate Justice of the Supreme Court; a fatally ambitious Roman ruler.

14. An insouciant jewel thief; a nightclub dancer fleeing from gangsters; one-third of an odd romantic triangle at a girls' school; a shrill, hysterical novelist jealous of her best friend; the heartless wife of a straying, disintegrating man.

Here's an extra question for no points, merely a tribute to one of the editor's favorite actresses:

Who played:

a gentle old lady separated from her husband and relegated to a home for the elderly; a senator's proud mother; the kindly head of an adoption home; the French-born maid in a Washington household; the hateful, tight-lipped matriarch of a Western family.

(Answers on page 185)

THE GOLDEN SILENCE

Here is a quiz celebrating some of the most famous performances given in silent films by leading players, some of whom went on successfully to sound.

In each instance, the character played by that performer is described. Name the performer *and* the film, scoring five points for each correct answer. (A score of 75 or more points should be commended.)

1. A fearless young man who kills a sea monster, goes through the Cavern of Fires, and rides a winged white horse.
2. A grasping, money-obsessed woman who is finally murdered by her desperate husband.
3. An abused French waif who has a poignant romance with a self-characterized "remarkable fellow."
4. A contemptible fake Russian count who seduces an envoy's wife.
5. A fisherman's spirited daughter who falls in love with the son of the nasty old man trying to evict the fisher-folk from their homes.
6. A young Chinese who befriends and falls in love with a mistreated girl.
7. A dashing English fashion-plate who ends up a broken old man in an asylum.
8. A flirtatious young girl, called the Little Disturber by the townspeople, who is caught up in the miseries of World War I.
9. A beautiful but conscienceless woman who inspires a deadly rivalry between two close friends.
10. A circus clown, in love with a count's daughter, who arranges for the death of the villainous baron who wants to marry her.
11. "Dangerous Diana," an irrepressible flapper who is actually a moral girl seeking true love.
12. A deafened musician who decides to devote his life to helping downtrodden people.
13. A meek, almost child-like man who helps a minister's blind daughter rout the law-breakers in the town.
14. An idolized toreador who is swept into an amorous adventure with a sultry woman.
15. A girl who becomes a nun when she believes her lover is dead, only to have him re-appear years later.
16. A luckless soul who finds himself trapped in a cage with a sleeping lion while a fox terrier barks noisily outside the cage.
17. A movie projectionist who is also an amateur sleuth.
18. A department-store clerk who is conned into climbing the side of a building.
19. A titled English girl, shipwrecked on an island, who falls in love with her butler.
20. A winsome French girl who clings to her doughboy lover as he marches off to war.

(Answers on page 185)

PROFESSIONALLY SPEAKING

This quiz deals with the screen's portrayal of professionals; the doctors, lawyers, teachers, nurses, actors, and writers who have waxed noble (and sometimes ignoble) in movies. No scoring on this quiz—just a test of memory.

Doctors

1. Who played the first Dr. Kildare in films, in a movie called *Internes Can't Take Money*?
2. Sultry Gloria Grahame usually meant trouble. Name the two films in which she meant trouble for doctors.
3. Who played Dr. George Ferguson in a 1934 hospital drama from MGM?
4. Name at least two actresses who have played doctors in films.
5. In a 1950 MGM movie (reportedly a financial disaster), Dr. Cary Grant performed an operation on dictator José Ferrer. What was the film's name?

Lawyers

1. The 1955 film *Trial* centered on an explosive murder trial of a Mexican youth. Who played the wily Communist lawyer who tries to manipulate the proceedings?
2. Name the 1951 film in which Spencer Tracy played a criminal lawyer who saves an innocent boy from execution.
3. In *Roxie Hart* (1942), who played Billy Flynn, the "simple, barefoot mouthpiece" who defends the flamboyant heroine?
4. Lawyer Howard Joyce speaking: "I don't want you to tell me anything except what is needed to save your neck." The movie? And who played Joyce?
5. Who played the chief prosecuting attorney in *Anatomy of a Murder*?

Teachers

Name the actor or actress who played the following teachers and the films in which they appeared:
1. Ella Bishop
2. Thackery
3. Richard Dadier
4. Nora Trinell
5. Professor Kingsfield

Nurses

1. Edith Cavell was a nurse who served heroically in World War I. Who played Nurse Cavell on the screen?
2. *Cry Havoc* was a 1943 film about nurses who served heroically in World War II. Name any three of the principal cast members.
3. In *Vigil in the Night* (1940), Carole Lombard played a nurse who takes the blame for her sister's fatal mistake. Who played her sister?
4. In MGM's Dr. Kildare series, was head nurse Molly Bird played by Elizabeth Risdon, Alma Kruger, or Lucile Watson?
5. Who played the sympathetic nurse who befriends Richard Todd in Warners' *The Hasty Heart* (1950)?

Actors

Who played each of the following fictional actors or actresses, and in which film?
1. Anthony John
2. Beatrice Page
3. Esther Blodgett (two actresses)
4. Sam Lawson
5. Lola Burns

Writers

Identify the actor or actress who played each of the following famous authors, and the film in which he/she appeared in the role:
1. Charlotte Brontë
2. Gustave Flaubert
3. F. Scott Fitzgerald
4. George Sand
5. W. Somerset Maugham

(Answers on page 185)

THEY HAD CHARACTER

Here is a photo quiz revolving about some of the best character actors of the thirties and forties. No scoring in this case, only questions that we hope will spur you to remember the great performers in films, most of whom have departed from the scene.

Photo 1

A scene from Frank Capra's 1933 film, *Lady For a Day*, in which Apple Annie, an old derelict transformed into a grand society lady, awaits the arrival of her daughter, while her friends look on. May Robson was Annie, but who played the befurred lady beside her? And who was the deadpanned actor with the top hat, standing at her other side?

Photo 2
The movie is Busby Berkeley's *Gold Diggers of 1933.* Yes, the gold digger watching Ginger Rogers and Guy Kibbee at play is none other than Aline MacMahon, years before she began playing benign and wise matriarchs. Ms. MacMahon had a lively career at Warners in the thirties. Question: in which film did she play a fake countess, otherwise known as "Barrelhouse Betty"?

Photo 3
Here is a scene from Warners' 1940 movie of World War I, *The Fighting 69th.* In a trench, Father Duffy (Pat O'Brien) is talking with Wild Bill Donovan (George Brent). You are asked to identify the reliable actor at the left. He has appeared in a great many films, but he is probably best remembered as the nasty male nurse in the alcoholic ward in *The Lost Weekend* (1945).

Photo 4
Here's Alan Hale displaying his molars for the benefit of son James Cagney in Warners' *The Strawberry Blonde* (1941). In which film did this durable actor play Errol Flynn's father? And in which movie did he play Ida Lupino's husband?

Photo 5
Identify the actor at the right in this scene with Paul Newman from *Somebody Up There Likes Me* (1956). Perhaps best remembered for his performance as Bernstein in Orson Welles' *Citizen Kane* (1941), he was also memorable as Rita Hayworth's jealous husband in *The Lady From Shanghai* (1948) and as the business tycoon in *Patterns* (1956).

Photo 6
Here is a scene from Columbia's 1932 film, *Washington Merry-Go-Round*, directed by James Cruze. It featured the distinguished stage actor at the right, in one of his first film roles. His name? (Two years later, he was irately in pursuit of daughter Claudette Colbert in *It Happened One Night*.) Another question: who is the overwrought actor pointing an accusing finger?

Photo 7
In this scene from *Arizona* (1940), Jean Arthur is holding her gun on a veteran character actor proficient at playing crooks, wretches, and low-down varmints. He made his debut in *The Thin Man* (1934), then went on to be despicable or weasel-like in *Mr. Smith Goes to Washington* (1939), *Sullivan's Travels* (1941), and many other films. What was his name?

Photo 8
In this photo from *Gilda* (1946), we have three fine character actors, one of them very dead. Name, respectively, the actors playing the bartender, the crouching policeman, and the corpse. (At the right, justifiably disturbed, are Glenn Ford and Rita Hayworth.)

Photo 9
While still in his twenties, Lee J. Cobb repeated his stage role in the 1939 filming of Clifford Odets' *Golden Boy*, playing William Holden's emotional Italian father. Holden made his film debut in the title role. But who is the actor standing between them in the photograph?

Photo 10
In this scene from *Whistling in the Dark* (1941), one of the screen's most persuasive villains is seen restraining Red Skelton who is holding Ann Rutherford. What was his name, and in which film was he (1) a satanic madman who holds Joan Crawford in his thrall and (2) a Nazi spy trapped by con-man Humphrey Bogart?

Photo 11

The fussy gentleman with Fred Astaire in this scene from *Top Hat* is, of course, the inimitable Edward Everett Horton. Here's a question for Horton fans: in a 1944 film, he gave one of his best but most uncharacteristic performances as a decadent count infatuated with Linda Darnell. What was the name of the film?

Photo 12

In this scene from *Central Park* (1932) Joan Blondell is talking to a young actor who went on to many character roles in movies. His last role, as Elizabeth Hartman's alcoholic grandfather in *A Patch of Blue* (1965), was one of his best. What was his name?

Photo 13

In this scene from *Wife, Husband and Friend*, Warner Baxter is giving the heave-ho to a veteran character actress who appeared in many films in the thirties and early forties. She played the title role in *Roberta* (1935), Shirley Temple's crusty but kind-hearted Aunt Miranda in *Rebecca of Sunnybrook Farm* (1938), and wise old Cousin Philippa in *Adam Had Four Sons* (1941). Her name?

Photo 14
Money matters are being discussed in this scene from *Gold Diggers of 1935.* The lady in the center was a noted actress who won a Supporting Actress Academy Award in 1938 for her perfomance as Mrs. O'Leary, the lady whose cow started the Great Chicago Fire. She was also addled Angelica Bullock in *My Man Godfrey (1936).* What was her name?

Photo 15
In this scene from Preston Sturges' *Hail the Conquering Hero* (1944), false hero Eddie Bracken is surrounded by his proud family and friends: (left to right) Freddie Steele, Georgia Caine, Ella Raines, and the marvelous character actress we are asking you to identify. She achieved perhaps her finest moment in films as the doughty and determined old lady in MGM's *Intruder in the Dust* (1949).

Photo 16
In Irving Berlin's *This Is the Army* (1943), Ronald Reagan weds Joan Leslie while proud fathers George Murphy and (guess who?) look on. This actor played largely diffident souls in the thirties and early forties, notably in *Love Me Tonight* (1932) and *The Moon's Our Home* (1936). His name?

Photo 17
In this scene from *Lost Honeymoon* (1947), who is the old codger at the right, standing with Ann Richards, Tom Conway, and Franchot Tone? (He was one of the screen's best old codgers.)

Photo 18
Sly landlord Mr. Appopolous is showing his ramshackle basement apartment to the unwary Sherwood girls (Rosalind Russell and Janet Blair) in *My Sister Eileen* (1942). Who played Appopolous, and who played the role in the 1955 musical version?

Photo 19
She forgave Gyppo Nolan, shrieked incessantly at the sight of the invisible man, waited on Maid Marian, and made her presence known without saying a word as Richard Haydn's old mother. Here she is being protective toward Brenda Marshall in a scene from *The Sea Hawk* (1940), with Alan Hale, Claude Rains, and Errol Flynn. Who was this grand actress?

Photo 20
In this scene from *The Corn Is Green* (1945), teacher Bette Davis speaks with student John Dall, while squire Nigel Bruce looks on. Standing humbly aside is the meek Miss Ronberry, played by a superb actress in her film debut. What is her name?

(Answers on page 186)

MOVIE MATTERS

Here, for your amusement and/or edification, are some thoughts by film people of a less than profound nature, along with some misguided reflections and aborted plans. They are from the pages of the British magazine, *Films and Filming*, in the late fifties and early sixties.

Our Dirty Movie Queens

Greta Garbo in a December, 1956 interview: "Time passes so quickly, too quickly. Ordinary things take so much time, there's none left for the extraordinary. Even just getting up in the morning takes so long. Would it not be better on the whole if we all went around dirty?"

Marlene Dietrich, on the set of *The Monte Carlo Story* (1957), claimed that she hates playing elegant women: "Give me a role where I can grovel in the dirt, then I'm happy. You have to work so much harder to convince the public you're suffering when your gloves and handbag match."

The Clouded Crystal Ball

Suzy Parker on a 1957 set: "The greatest thrill of my life is at last being able to *talk* in front of a camera. They've got me for seven years and I intend to never shut up in that time."

Marlon Brando speaking in 1959: "Protest can become a way of life. There's that danger present in the manifestations of the Beat Generation. . . . Sometimes when protest is carried to an extreme, you can't help thinking that if everybody was changed to conform with what these people say they want, they still might not know what to do. . . . Mere protest for its own sake can be a foolish thing. After a while, they may lose sight of what they were protesting about."

In 1959, asked about his reactions to critics, Alfred Hitchcock remarked: "Well, they may not like my work so much now. You see, I'm no longer being discovered."

Words of Wisdom from the Movie World

Kirk Douglas: "To what extent could a film be called artistic? If, for two hours, it can get them [the audience] away from their troubles, then it must be a major artistic contribution." (1958)

Maurice Chevalier (at age 71): "Now I have to appeal to a new generation. Method? No. Technique? A little. But all an artist really needs to succeed is sincerity." (1959)

Producer Joe Levine on *Sodom and Gomorrah*: "The moment I heard the title I knew this would be a great film." (1961)

George Stevens, on casting John Wayne in *The Greatest Story Ever Told*: "John Wayne is a giant in the film world. His contribution will be a cornerstone for this monumental task. . . . Each of the memorable figures from Biblical history will be enacted by a great artiste because each role is so dramatic and inspiring as to demand the contributions of the world's finest performers." (1960)

In the background: John Wayne as a Roman soldier in THE GREATEST STORY EVER TOLD (1965). With Max von Sydow as Jesus

Producer Samuel Bronston was asked why he had cast Jeffrey Hunter as Christ in *King of Kings*: "Because we thought he was right for the part. Everything about him was right. His private life as well. We had him investigated." (1961)

Tony Curtis and Marilyn Monroe in the yacht scene from SOME LIKE IT HOT (1959)

Think Big

In 1955 Jack Warner announced a million-dollar production of *Faust* in CinemaScope, using Goethe's drama and Gounod's music. Mentioned for Mephistopheles were Jerome Hines, Ezio Pinza, and Jack Palance. Likely contender for Faust: Mario Lanza. Opera stars Eleanor Steber and Nadine Conner were vying for the role of Marguerite.

In 1957 Darryl F. Zanuck planned a film on the life of Josef Stalin. He stated: "I offered Khrushchev a screen credit but I haven't heard from him." Yul Brynner and James Mason were candidates for the title role.

In 1959 Jerry Wald acquired the rights to Fidel Castro's life story. He had definite views on casting: Marlon Brando for the title role and Frank Sinatra as his brother Raoul. Castro indicated that he would like Ernest Hemingway to write the script.

Early in 1960 Frank Capra was considering a film on the life of St. Paul. He suggested Frank Sinatra for the title role: "This is not so odd when you remember what kind of man Paul was when he started out—a heel."

The Directors Speak

Sidney J. Furie: "I hope I can put over in my films the idea that there is no need to be disillusioned about life. There are good things, some of the time; and it is the good things that are worth seeking—and making films about." (1958)

Frank Capra: "I'm not sure to which extent 'art' has a place in filmmaking. The medium is certainly capable of producing art, but I don't think it's really there. We make pictures primarily to entertain. The Europeans have a different point of view, but I think they're off base. Films are not pictures that have to be hung on the wall. . . ." (1958)

Cecil B. DeMille on his bathroom scenes: "In my boyhood, there was a tin bath in a small dark cupboard. The eldest son used the water first and the other children followed him. I decided I would show people what a bathroom should be like. After all, we spend a lot of time there." (1957)

Billy Wilder on the Tony Curtis-Marilyn Monroe yacht scene in *Some Like It Hot*: "You know, Curtis said 'Oh, boy' at the start of the first take. By the time we reached take 30, he was a little worn . . . it's rather like eating too much chocolate." (1959)

Charlie Chaplin: "I'd rather see a man stir his teacup with a spoon than see a volcano erupting. I want my camera to be like the proscenium of a theatre, come close to the actor, not lose his contour, bring the audience to him. Economy of action has gone through all my work." (1957)

More from Frank Capra: "Each individual possesses the mental and spiritual equipment to overcome adversity. . . . Isn't, after all, the finest entertainment the entertainment that is uplifting?" (1959)

Who, Me?

In 1955 Clark Gable wrote in a series of articles that he made his film debut as an extra in *Bird of Paradise*,

THE PAINTED DESERT (1931). With Helen Twelvetrees, J. Farrell MacDonald, and Clark Gable

released in 1932. He was wrong. By 1932, he had already appeared in at least a dozen films. He made his film debut as a cowboy in *The Painted Desert* (1931).

Marlene Dietrich has also been known to deny the facts about her early career. She has repeatedly claimed that her first film was *The Blue Angel*, but she had appeared in German films as early as 1925. (She had a role in a Greta Garbo silent film, *The Joyless Street*.)

Department of Dubious Correlations:

Composer Miklos Rosza: "In the last century, the composer wrote opera and oratorio. In the twentieth century, film composition has taken over." (1960)

The Best-Laid Plans

Here are some film plans from the mid-fifties that either came to naught or changed substantially before taking final form.

Greer Garson was going to play Gertrude Lawrence in a film biography. (Julie Andrews ultimately played the role in the 1970 film, *Star!*.)

In 1955 Ann Miller was talking about a new film version of *The Women*, with Joan Crawford, Rosalind Russell (of the original cast), and Eleanor Parker. It was to have "some songs." (A musical version, *The Opposite Sex*, was released the following year, but Crawford, Russell, and Parker were not in it. The cast included June Allyson, Joan Collins, Dolores Gray—and Ann Miller.)

Van Johnson was assigned to co-star with Judy Holliday in the film version of *The Solid Gold Cadillac*. The role finally went to Paul Douglas.

Nathaniel Benchley was going to write the screenplay for *Melville Goodwin, U.S.A.*, based on the J. P. Marquand novel and starring Humphrey Bogart and Lauren Bacall. The movie was finally released as *Top Secret Affair* with Kirk Douglas and Susan Hayward in the leading roles. The screenplay was by Roland Kibbee and Allan Scott.

Looking to cast the title role in *The Helen Morgan Story*, Warners tested Jennifer Jones, Shelley Winters, and Susan Hayward. The role went to Ann Blyth.

The last Hardy family film, *Andy Hardy Comes Home*, was to be followed by a movie called *Andy Hardy Carries On*. He never did.

In 1958 Mae West was scheduled to return to the screen in *Klondike Lou*, and Danny Kaye was set to play in a Columbia comedy, *The Bamboo Kid*, about an American movie star involved in the Far Eastern underworld. Both plans came to naught.

The film version of Ray Lawler's play, *The Summer of the Seventeenth Doll*, was set to co-star Burt Lancaster and Rita Hayworth. It was released in 1960 under

SEASON OF PASSION (1960). With Anne Baxter, Ernest Borgnine, Angela Lansbury, and John Mills

the title *Season of Passion*, with Ernest Borgnine, Anne Baxter, John Mills, and Angela Lansbury.

Spring 1961: William Thackeray's *Vanity Fair* was switched by writer Gavin Lambert from the England of the 1800s to the southern United States as a vehicle for Marilyn Monroe.

TWO:
ALL ABOUT FILMS

In this section, we concentrate on the movies themselves, talking about some of the wonderfully foolish and endearing lore about films, jogging and challenging your memory about movies old and not so old, offering quizzes on which you can test your standing in the community of buffs.

We're starting with Howard Thompson's article on forgotten movies. It may inspire you to think of the movies *you* remember—and wish you could see again. . . .

FORGOTTEN MOVIES

By Howard Thompson

Where is *Menace*, a superior thriller released in 1934?

They showed it on television in New York City about fifteen years ago. But where is it now? I miss it. And if they still have *Menace* in the television vaults, why don't they dust it off instead of wearing out *Suspicion*?

There are many movies, like old friends, I would enjoy seeing again. These pictures haunt me—stuck in my mind like a cavalcade of mini-trailers (the old theatre previews of coming attractions).

Several of the movies mentioned here can indeed be found if you live in New York City, which currently has the world's most bountiful smorgasbord of vintage films. They are now cresting on a tidal wave of nostalgia, surfacing all over town, from museum to theatre mousehole. The trick, as you squint at a mile-long listing of theatres through a magnifying glass, is to find one of these treasures that fits your working schedule.

Some movies I would like to see again are stashed away temporarily because of remakes and copyrights. Some may be privately owned; some undoubtedly are lost. But it's the ones I can't forget and remember pleasurably, often vaguely, that fan my frustration. One way to be sure

you're not having an hallucination is to flip open the *Film Daily Year Book* (a fat but totable tome) and match a hallowed film title with the year of release. It's the only way to be sure you haven't imagined the picture out of a film buff's cluttered memory.

In my case, because of lifelong moviemania, verifying the year is even more frustrating, since I can also generally recall where I saw the movie and what my life was at the time.

Hence *Menace,* which I saw as an impressionable child at the Paramount Theatre in a Tennessee mountain town named Bristol on a Monday afternoon after flunking a math exam, as usual.

It was a first-rate thriller, with a provocative title and a neat plot. For years snippets of *Menace* flashed through my mind, especially that opening—a plane winging through a tropical storm, a lightning crackle that split a huge dam, and four colonists at a bridge table—a game that triggered a series of revenge murders. The butler, Halliwell Hobbes, *didn't* do it, although it seemed that he had, until the very end. The heroine, a woman I loved throughout adolescence, was the toothsome Gertrude

MENACE (1934). With Halliwell Hobbes and Gertrude Michael

THE GREENE MURDER CASE (1929). With Jean Arthur and Eugene Pallette

Michael, who still looks attractive on television as the friendly waitress in *Flamingo Road*, one of her last parts.

Now for an obvious one. Where, oh where is *Kitty Foyle* (1940), the film for which Ginger Rogers won an Oscar? Much as I'd like to see this, I'd rather catch *In Person* (1935), a minor but pleasant movie in which she sang three good tunes composed by Oscar Levant (the best was "Don't Mention Love to Me") and performed a funny bit wearing a buck-toothed disguise as a movie queen dodging autograph fans. And even more than *In Person*, I'd like to see *Primrose Path* (1940), reportedly her favorite—a bleak-edged romantic comedy with Joel McCrea, Marjorie Rambeau and little Joan Carroll—based on a wonderfully grimy play by Robert L. Buckner and Walter Hart. Surprisingly, this dealt with a family that has been pursuing the world's oldest profession for generations, until Ginger breaks the line by reforming. And where is the sophisticated Ginger spicery called *Star of Midnight* (1935), with William Powell as a debonair lawyer suspected of murdering a gossip columnist and Rogers as his persistent girlfriend?

But let's hop back to the mystery-suspense bracket. It's probable that television's Perry Mason forced the shelving of Warners' Perry Mason movies of the early thirties that had Warren William as the lawyer-sleuth. They were adequate—nothing more. The series I *am* curious about is the group of movies based on the S. S. Van Dine novels about detective Philo Vance. I saw four as a tender bud: *The Greene Murder Case* (1929), *The Bishop Murder Case* (1930), *The Dragon Murder Case*

(1934)—not sci-fi but swimming-pool mayhem—and the first and possibly the best, *The Canary Murder Case* (1929).* In that film I recall Louise Brooks as a plumed and feathered showgirl cavorting on a stage swing. Quite a lot has been made of the Brooks image in nostalgic print in recent years. I believe—and sincerely hope—this intriguing lady is still alive. The memory of that picture certainly is.

But I recall more clearly a young, baby-faced Jean Arthur in *The Greene Murder Case*. It was a shock to me, as a child, to learn that a woman could turn out to be a killer; I can still hear her squealing fiercely—yes, with the same buzz-saw edge in her voice—as she either sailed out of the window or off a roof at the end. How I'd love to see young Jean do her evil thing again from way back!

For that matter, where's a hard-breathing old 1930 melodrama called *The Silver Horde*, with Miss Arthur, Joel McCrea and Evelyn Brent involved in romance and salmon-fishing in Alaska? I still recall a showdown when McCrea, disillusioned, snarls at Jean: "Why, you're nothing but a _____." And here the camera quickly cuts to eavesdropping Evelyn, whose mouth falls open. Oh, for

* Editor's Note: There were a number of Philo Vance mystery films in the thirties, with the detective played at various times by William Powell, Warren William, Basil Rathbone, James Stephenson, Edmund Lowe, Wilfrid Hyde-White and even Paul Lukas. Vance continued into the forties.

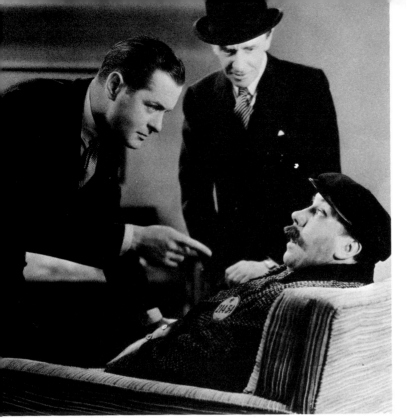

THE MYSTERY OF MR. X (1934). With Robert Montgomery, Ivan Simpson, and Forrester Harvey

the power of suggestion inadvertently caused by the good old censors!

Has anybody heard these suspense titles mentioned in years: *Double Door, Miss Fane's Baby Is Stolen, The Mystery of Mr. X*, and *College Scandal*?

I remember *Double Door* (1934) as a well-reviewed adaptation of a Broadway play about the inhabitants of a gloomy Gothic mansion. There was a secret chamber into which a grim-looking actress named Mary Morris, as the mad old mistress of the house, lured doe-eyed Evelyn Venable, the bride of Miss Morris' half-brother, Kent Taylor. (The movie marked two debuts: Charles Vidor as director and Anne Revere in a repetition of her stage role as Miss Morris' sister.)

I can still hear the accented voice of the lovely German actress, Dorothea Wieck, in *Miss Fane's Baby Is Stolen* (1934), as a Hollywood movie queen who pleads over the radio ("Thees ees Mad-e-line Fane") for the return of her kidnaped infant, Baby LeRoy. (The plot must have pleased W. C. Fields, down the street at Paramount.) And what a climax! The kidnap gang, hiding their prize in an isolated shack, has not expected a visit from a friendly, warmhearted and inquisitive neighbor—Alice Brady, even better here than in her Oscar-winning role as Mrs. O'Leary in *In Old Chicago*. As I recall, she accidentally brushes dye (shoe polish) off the child's blonde locks, sees the light, grabs the toddler, and roars off in her old Model T Ford, holding Baby LeRoy in her aproned lap, with the gang in hot pursuit.

I remember, and always will, the chase climax of *College Scandal* (1935), especially the horrible, fixed expression of Mary Nash, as she drives to her doom in her nightgown, her bare feet jamming the accelerator. It turned out that Mary had carefully stalked her dead son's fraternity brothers for years. Why? Because they had tied him to a graveyard tombstone one night—and the boy's heart had stopped beating. I also recall Arline Judge sashaying around the campus; the picture also had a good tune, "In the Middle of a Kiss," but it had no business in a thriller.

The Mystery of Mr. X (1934) was a first-class whodunit with Robert Montgomery as a Scotland Yard sleuth and Elizabeth Allan as his aristocratic fiancée. And what a denouement here, with Montgomery staring at a large, crime-spot marker map of London. Who is this Mr. X, and how can he go on killing so many policemen and remain undetected? Where will he strike next?

Aha—Bob has it! With two chalk slashes across the crime spots, he has drawn an incomplete X, indicating the next area to be struck. He realizes that the maniac-killer has been disguised as a London bobby. I recall the final trackdown vigil, with Montgomery dressed as a cop, standing next to a deserted warehouse wall, when suddenly a murderous hiss sends a rapier thrusting past his ear.

Film versions of well-known novels turn up repeatedly, but where are some of the versions of Sinclair Lewis's tales of Middle America? Does anyone recall that his classic *Main Street* became a very good movie under the vapid title of *I Married a Doctor* (1936), with, of all people, Pat O'Brien and Josephine Hutchinson as the small-town doctor and his big-city bride? There was also a lively version of *Babbitt* (1934), with Guy Kibbee and Aline MacMahon, and a surprisingly interesting version of *Ann Vickers* (1933), with Irene Dunne as an ardent social reformer, Walter Huston as the judge who loves her, and Edna May Oliver as a doctor whose name is branded forever in my memory: Malvina Wormser.

Speaking of Miss Dunne, there was an excellent film derived from Sidney Howard's *The Silver Cord* (1933). Miss Dunne was fine as the intrepid wife who had dared to pry her husband, Joel McCrea, from his dragon mama, Laura Hope Crews (repeating her stage performance in her juiciest movie role of all). But Frances Dee wasn't so lucky, losing her weaker husband, Eric Linden, to his mother and hysterically flinging herself into an icy river. The fadeout, with mother and son left alone, was memorable. And where is the Irene Dunne-John Boles vehicle neatly culled in 1934 from Edith Wharton's novel, *The Age of Innocence*?

Many early Bette Davis films are around now. But where is a 1933 charmer called *The Working Man*, with Bette as the spoiled ward of George Arliss, playing a rich tycoon who poses as one of his factory employees. As for that great, missed artist, where are the other films displaying his ripe acting style: *The Green Goddess* (1930), *Alexander Hamilton* (1931), *Voltaire* (1933), and *Cardinal Richelieu* (1935), with a beautiful musical score?

Where are all those Constance Bennett rags-to-riches (or vice versa) sagas? I especially liked *Bed of Roses* (1933), with Connie and a snappy Pert Kelton as tarts cruising up and down the Mississippi River and Miss Bennett's finally shedding a lavish penthouse for the honest love of a stalwart riverboat pilot, Joel McCrea. Is there some law—or simply a technicality—preventing the showing of Deanna Durbin's films on television? My favorite is *Mad About Music* (1938), with pert young Deanna as a movie star's child hidden away in a Swiss boarding school. It had a grand opening, with the girls biking down a road singing "I Love to Whistle"—and Helen Parrish as the resident meanie. "Why do you dislike me?" Deanna asks her calmly. Helen retorts, "I don't dislike you—I hate you."

Where's a forgotten little musical called *Turn Off the Moon* (1937), with Charles Ruggles, Eleanore Whitney,

and Johnny Downs, a neat plot spoofing astrology, and a batch of lilting tunes by Sam Coslow? Another I miss is the charming, rather quiet musical based on the wartime perseverance of London's Windmill Theatre, titled *Tonight and Every Night* (1945). The leads were Rita Hayworth, Janet Blair, Marc Platt and Lee Bowman.

There are two old English-made musicals I'd give my soul to see: *Chu Chin Chow* (1934), with Fritz Kortner and Anna May Wong, reportedly a fine filming of the long-run stage operetta about Ali Baba and the Forty Thieves; and *Bitter Sweet* (1933), with Anna Neagle and Fernand Gravey (later Gravet), which I understand was every bit as lovely as the Jeanette MacDonald-Nelson Eddy version was dreadful. And has the Jessie Matthews musical, *It's Love Again* (1936), gone for good? I can still see her—and those magnificent legs—and a suave partner doing a stunning "temple dance" atop a platform the size of a dime.* And whatever happened to the

* The *New York Times* review (May 23, 1936) said that the dance was "a blend of travelogue Bali, pre-Repeal Charleston, and late Harlem truckin'. Very good, too."

BIRD OF PARADISE (1932). With Joel McCrea and Dolores Del Rio

delightful British movie of *Blithe Spirit* (1945), Noel Coward's play about a ghostly marital triangle, with Rex Harrison, Constance Cummings, Kay Hammond, and a wondrously funny Margaret Rutherford as the medium, Madame Arcati? Although not a musical, the picture had a striking background score and a lilting waltz theme by Richard Addinsell, who composed the "Warsaw Concerto."

One of the great screen beauties of the twenties and thirties was Mexican-born Dolores Del Rio. Who could ever forget her in that luscious, early *Bird of Paradise* (1932)? She played a South Seas maiden rescued from a volcano and other disasters by Joel McCrea. She also made a surprisingly effective *Madame Du Barry* (1934), in which King Louis XV (Reginald Owen) powdered Versailles with sugar because his mistress "missed the snow." I can still see and hear her at the fadeout, walking away, beautifully gowned and murmuring a little song, slower and slower, as a prelude to incoming, grim history: "The king of France. . . ."

Why didn't French actress Danielle Darrieux immediately click in Hollywood as *The Rage of Paris* (1938), a genuinely amusing, frothy comedy in which she appeared opposite Douglas Fairbanks, Jr., with a fine supporting cast headed by Mischa Auer and Helen Broderick? I miss *Sequoia* (1934), a beautifully photographed movie of wildlife in the California mountains, with performances by a deer and a puma that outdistanced the human players (Jean Parker, Russell Hardie). I also miss the trenchantly Southern *Carolina* (1934), expanded from Paul Green's play, *The House of Connelly*. It was one of Janet Gaynor's best films in which she played a winsome Northern intruder opposite Robert Young and that marvelous veteran actress, Henrietta Crosman. And in an entirely different vein, where is *Hitler's Children* (1943), a tragic, appealing war drama with Bonita Granville and Tim Holt? I happened to catch it at Fort Benning, Georgia, as a paratrooper in training.

I miss Katharine Hepburn's memorable hillbilly-tomboy, *Spitfire* (1934), with Robert Young and Ralph Bellamy, from Lula Vollmer's play, *Sun-Up*. Ditto a clever comedy, *The Perfect Specimen* (1937), with Errol Flynn as a "scientifically" reared millionaire and Joan Blondell as a girl who introduces him to the real world. Also an amusing satire, *The Idle Rich* (1929), pairing ZaSu Pitts and Edna May Oliver, with a very funny dinner scene almost matching the classic one in *Alice Adams*. Even as I write this, I've suddenly recalled—out of nowhere—two genuine, forgotten pearls from the past: Marie Dressler in *The Late Christopher Bean* (1934), a touching drama about a humble servant and a dead artist in New England, based on the Sidney Howard play; and *The Pursuit of Happiness*, from a play by Lawrence Langner and Armina Marshall, an utterly charming comedy of the

HARD TO HANDLE (1933). With Ruth Donnelly, James Cagney and Mary Brian

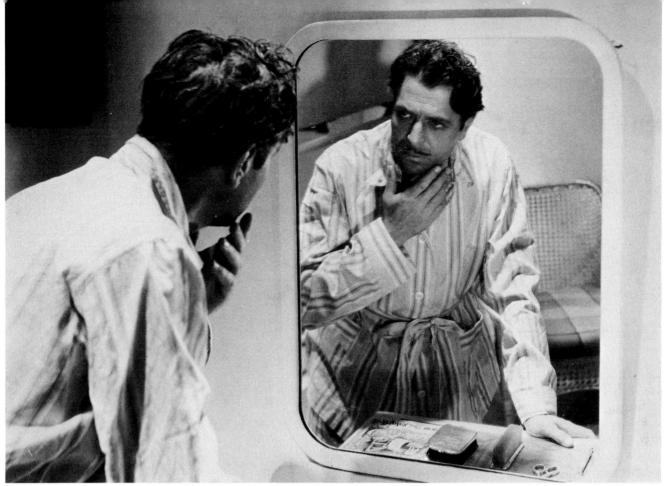

GRAND CANARY (1934). With Warner Baxter

American Revolutionary War, with Francis Lederer as a visiting Hessian soldier, Joan Bennett as a smitten New England daughter, and Mary Boland and Charles Ruggles as her parents.

Then there was a Jimmy Cagney comedy, *Hard to Handle* (1933), with Mary Brian and the inimitably sharp-tongued Ruth Donnelly. I remember so well the scene in which our hero, a dynamo con man and sharpie, gets a dignified society matron to endorse a jar of cold cream. With the photographers ready to snap her holding the jar, she says, "Just a minute, just a minute, young man," and Cagney bounds over innocently. She continues, "How much am I getting to sell this axle grease?"

It took a recent trip to New Orleans and a boat ride down the Mississippi to realize how much I've missed one of Will Rogers' best vehicles, *Steamboat Round the Bend* (1935), released after his death. Directed by John Ford, it was, to my recollection, a richly atmospheric and pungent movie about a good-natured medicine man (Rogers) who races his rattletrap steamboat against his rival (Irvin S. Cobb). And where *are* all the old Rogers comedies, such as *David Harum* (1934), *Judge Priest* (1934), and *Doubting Thomas* (1935)? If only television would revive these and squash those elephantine Eddie Cantor farces from the Goldwyn studio!

I never pass a certain Fifth Avenue mansion, near the Metropolitan Museum, without looking up at the top floors and recalling *The Match King* (1932), a fine drama featuring Warren William's best performance as a thinly disguised Ivar Kreuger, the international, Swedish-born swindler. The cast included the forgotten Juliette Compton as a none-too-good girl smitten by the Match King's roguish charm.

And speaking of *her*, it took a trip several years ago to the Canary Islands, out into the Atlantic off Casablanca, for me to remember *Grand Canary* (1934) after all these years. I drew some odd looks that night while dining alone near the main square of Palmas and suddenly yelping "Oh, yes!" to myself in rather loud English.

Yes, good old *Grand Canary*, that quietly atmospheric romance, from the novel by A. J. Cronin. I can still recall a steamer pulling into the exotic islands carrying Warner Baxter as a disillusioned doctor, the golden-haired, sweet-faced Madge Evans, and the raven-haired Miss Compton. Where is it now?

For movie buffs, the chance to see these and many other forgotten films of the past would be a boon and a blessing. For the moment, however, they remain largely in limbo, awaiting re-discovery. And we buffs can rely on only the deepest reaches of memory.

SONGS, DANCES,
AND SNAPPY SAYINGS

Here is a quiz to test your knowledge of those toe-tapping, eye-popping, heart-warming film musicals most movie buffs cherish. A score of 80 or more shows that you can sing along with the experts.

I. For three points each, name the movie musical evoked by each of the following:

a. The Alhambra Café. "It's a Great Big World." "The Train Must Be Fed."

b. "Love In Bloom." Mrs. Moss Hart. *How To Be Very, Very Popular.*

c. Claire Luce. "Let's K-nock K-nees." "Your wife ezza safe weeth Tonetti. He prefersa da spaghetti."

d. "Let's Go Slumming." The Ritz Brothers. "The pretty young brunette on the pink *Police Gazette.*"

e. "Spring, Spring, Spring." Stephen Vincent Benét. Michael Kidd.

f. "He Loves and She Loves." "Emphaticalism." Maggie Prescott.

g. The Girl from Brooklyn. "All of a Sudden My Heart Sings." Dean Stockwell.

h. Lucifer, Jr. "Life's Full of Consequences." Vernon Duke.

i. "Pay the Two Dollars." A suave jewel thief and his beautiful victim. "Love is like a burning ember."

j. Cousin Lily. "Weary Blues." "Well, spring isn't everything, is it, Essie?"

II. Often movie musicals, even mediocre ones, contain moments that filmgoers remember with pleasure. For three points each, name the film in which each of the following moments appear, all personal favorites of mine:

a. Virginia O'Brien sings a dead-pan version of the Latin-accented "Take It Easy."

b. Bobby Van performs an exhilarating dance, consisting mainly of a series of hopping steps across town.

c. Carmen Miranda, her fruit-basket hat bobbing on her head, invites us all to meet her at "Sloppy Joe's."

d. Ruby Keeler dances with Lee Dixon across giant typewriter keys.

e. Reginald Gardiner, a park policeman, suddenly launches into a wild impression of a symphony conductor leading an imaginary orchestra.

f. Ethel Merman performs a full-throated rendition of Irving Berlin's "Heat Wave."

g. Shirley Temple, Guy Kibbee, and Slim Summerville join in a take-off of the then-popular operatic aria in movie musicals.

h. Jimmy Durante belts out the song, "Toscanini, Iturbi, and Me."

i. Appearing abruptly in the middle of the musical, Louis Armstrong joins Bing Crosby for a Cole Porter tune, "Now You Has Jazz."

j. Irene Dunne sings Jerome Kern's lovely "The Folks Who Live on the Hill" to Randolph Scott.

III. Here are some musical numbers from *non-musical* films. Can you identify the films, for two points each?

a. Hoagy Carmichael sings about "a very unfortunate colored man."

b. At a bar, Bette Davis and the resident chanteuse sing "Give Me Time for Tenderness."

c. Desperate for a drink, Claire Trevor pushes her way through a ragged chorus of "Moanin' Low."

d. David Wayne composes and sings "Farewell, Amanda" as a tribute to Katharine Hepburn.

e. Marlene Dietrich sings about "you and your 'eyes-across-the-table' technique."

f. Irene Dunne sings "I'll Get By" tenderly to her pilot lover, Spencer Tracy.

g. Looking ravishingly beautiful, Zsa Zsa Gabor descends a staircase, singing "Where Is Your Heart?".

h. Angela Lansbury sings a plaintive "Goodbye, Little Yellow Bird," in a rowdy English music hall.

i. Ida Lupino, at a piano, sings a torchy rendition of "One For My Baby."

j. Girl-on-the-skids Anne Baxter sings "Mam'selle" in a Paris bistro.

IV. Here is a question devoted entirely to the master of the film musical, Fred Astaire. Each answer is worth two points:

a. In which movie did Astaire sing "Music Makes Me?"

b. In the musical number, "Oh, Them Dudes," who was Astaire's singing and dancing partner?

c. Astaire and Rogers danced to "the Carioca," "the Maxixe," "the Yam," and others. But which of their dances was to a song "written by a Latin/A gondolier who sat in/His home out in Brooklyn/and gazed at the stars"?

d. Who were Astaire's partners in a memorable musical number at an English county fair "fun house" in *A Damsel in Distress*?

e. An officious waiter. A supercilious valet. The unctuous manager of a dance school. An irate hotel manager.

Who played all these roles in Astaire-Rogers musicals? (No points but a cheer of "Bravo!" if you can name the four films.)

f. In which film did Astaire play the role Bob Hope had done in the stage version? What was the role?

g. Name the two films in which Astaire died.

h. In which movie did Astaire dance on the walls and ceilings? (Hint: in this film, Keenan Wynn played twin brothers.)

i. In *Roberta*, Astaire declared "I Won't Dance." In which movie did he state "Never Gonna Dance"?

j. Astaire never danced on screen with Greta Garbo, but what is the movie connection between them?

(Answers on page 186)

Fred Astaire defies the law of gravity.

THE ILLS THAT FLESH IS HEIR TO

Film characters, like the human beings they sometimes resemble, are subject to all sorts of afflictions, from alcoholism to drug addiction, from social disorientation to rampant insanity.

Below are twenty case histories from movies, briefly summarized. For each one, name the film in which the case history figured, and the actor or actress who played the role. (Score five points for each correct answer—three each for the film and two each for the player.)

1. Virginia. Young married woman. Deeply psychotic. Under treatment by Dr. Mark Kik. Therapy includes electroshock treatment, hydrotherapy, narcosynthesis. Prognosis clouded.

2. Don. Thirties, writer. Acute alcoholism has resulted in violent hallucinations, severe anxiety. Possibly suicidal.

3. Ed. Schoolteacher with wife and son. Admitted to hospital suffering from addiction to cortisone, administered originally to arrest disease.

4. Frankie. Resident of Chicago slum area. Married to bedridden woman. Confirmed drug addict desperately in need of help. Has returned to drugs after one attempt at cure.

5. Francesca. Celebrated concert pianist. Has attempted suicide. Narco-hypnosis by Dr. Larsen has exposed deep-seated complexes, centering on her teacher and mentor, Nicholas.

6. Rhoda. Eight years old. Displays oddly rigid personality, becomes violently angry when opposed. Possibly dangerous.

7. Katrin. Young wife and mother. Deeply alcoholic since marriage to Joe, who is also alcoholic. Attempts at rehabilitation only temporarily successful to date. Jim, member of Alcoholics Anonymous, rendering assistance, but prognosis poor.

8. Joan. Young married woman. Admitted to psychopathic ward after severe breakdown. Suffers from uncontrollable mania for gambling. Husband urgently summoned.

9. J. B. Amnesiac. Posing as psychiatrist. Deeply disturbed by lapse of memory and by suspicion he may have committed murder. Therapy by Dr. Peterson uncovers traumatic experience in childhood.

10. "Doc." Middle-aged chiropractor. Confirmed alcoholic for many years. Attempted cure with aid of wife Lola, but cumulation of problems, marital and other, have produced setback. Prognosis tentatively hopeful at best.

11. Johnny. Young Korean veteran. Severe drug addict, committed to hospital for cure by distraught wife. Patient's brother has tried to help but failed repeatedly.

12. Louise. Professional nurse. Diagnosed as schizophrenic. Discovered wandering streets, muttering unintelligibly. Police investigating identity of "David" for whom patient claims to be looking.

13. Catherine. Hospitalized as severely disturbed. Possibility of lobotomy raised by doctors in consultation with girl's aunt. Questioning by psychiatrist suggests impact of shattering experience involving girl's cousin.

14. Terry. Tense, cold, arrogant young woman in need of psychiatric treatment. Suspect in murder case, along with twin sister Ruth, who appears more composed.

15. Lillian. Professional entertainer. Confirmed alcoholic, finally seeking help. Preliminary discussions reveal problems with ambitious mother, several wrecked marriages as contributing factors.

16. Nell. Young woman held for psychiatric tests and observation after threatening life of child for whom she was baby-sitting. Man claims she mistook him for her deceased boyfriend.

17. Jim. Convicted of attempt to molest young child. Released from prison and now under care of Irish psychiatrist, Dr. Edmund McNally. Has developed mature relationship with a widow named Ruth Leighton.

18. Patient (name withheld). Deeply disturbed, requires extensive therapy. Questioning reveals violently racist attitudes, membership in American Nazi party. Treatment by doctor uncovers sordid, painful childhood.

19. Jim. Teen-ager. Resident of Los Angeles, with well-to-do parents. Involved with friends in incidents outside the law, including so-called "chicky run" with stolen automobiles. Relationship with teen-age girl promises hope for improved future.

20. Jim. Baseball player. Confined to hospital after mental breakdown. Prolonged therapy indicates hard-driving, possessive father as determining factor in breakdown.

(Answers on page 187)

"AND I QUOTE . . ."

Here are fifty quotations from well-known movies. How many can you identify? Hint: The photographs on these pages are from films quoted in this quiz. But we're not saying which films. Score two points for each correct answer. (A score of 86 points or more should be commended.)

1. "Never be jealous again. Never doubt that I love you more than the world. More than myself."
2. "Can't wipe us out. Can't lick us. We'll go on forever. 'Cause we're the people."
3. "Gentlemen, you can't fight in here. This is the War Room!"
4. "Fred C. Dobbs don't say nothin' he don't mean."
5. "We're fighting for this woman's honor, which is more than *she* ever did."
6. "Men like my father cannot die. They are with me still—real in memory as they were real in flesh—loving and beloved forever."
7. "Frankie! Frankie! Your mother forgives me!"
8. "I'll live to see you—all of you—hang from the highest yardarm in the British fleet!"
9. "It's straight down the line for both of us!"
10. "I steal!"
11. "The bottom is loaded with nice people. Only cream and bastards rise."
12. "If what they feel for each other is even half of what *we* felt, then that is everything."
13. "It was Beauty killed the Beast!"
14. "Jungle Red, Sylvia!"
15. "I ain't so tough!"
16. "Darling, you're a mess. You should lay off the candy bars."
17. "Do me a favor, Harry. Drop dead."
18. "May I kiss your symmetrical digits?"
19. "Papa, my cup runneth over."
20. "Our bodies are earth. Our thoughts are clay. And we sleep and eat with death."
21. "Well, Sir, here we are again."
22. "There's not much meat on her, but what there is is *cherce*!"
23. "I'm legally dead and they're legally murderers. That I'm alive is not their fault. But I know 'em. I know lots of 'em. And they'll hang for it."
24. "I'm only a poor corrupt official."
25. "I'm the finest woman who ever walked the streets."
26. "For the woman the kiss—for the man the sword!"
27. "I don't know how to kiss or I would kiss you. Where do the noses go?"

66

28. "I'm going to stay right here and fight for this lost cause!"

29. "We've been shaken out of the magnolias."

30. "I'm still big. It's the pictures that got small."

31. "Mr. Allnut, dear."

32. "These are tears of gratitude. An old maid's gratitude. Nobody has ever called me 'darling' before."

33. "Made it, Ma. Top o' the world!"

34. "Hello, gorgeous."

35. "The only thing missing is the bloodhounds snapping at her rear end!"

36. "Behold the walls of Jericho! Maybe not as thick as the ones Joshua blew down with his trumpet but a lot safer."

37. "What does it matter if an individual is shattered if only Justice is resurrected?"

38. "You're probably in the wickedest, most corrupt, most godless city in America. Sometimes it frightens me."

39. "I hope they don't hang you, precious, by that sweet neck."

40. "Shut up and deal."

41. "Madness . . . madness! . . ."

42. "I could have had class. I could have been a contender."

43. "One Rocco more or less isn't worth dying for."

44. "Your general appearance is not distasteful."

45. "You've nothing to stay for. You've nothing to live for, really, have you. Look down there. It's easy, isn't it. Why don't you?"

46. "This is not only a war of soldiers in uniform. It is a war of the people—of all the people—and it must be fought not only on the battlefield but in the cities and in the villages, in the factories and on the farms, in the home and in the heart of every man, woman and child who loves freedom."

47. "Mass killing. Does not the world encourage it? I am an amateur by comparison."

48. "O-lan, you are the earth . . ."

49. "So they call me 'Concentration Camp' Ehrhardt!"

50. "The *Torrin*'s gone. Now she lies in 1,500 fathoms and with most of her shipmates. They lie in very good company with the ship we love."

(*Answers on page 187*)

THE MOVIE SCENE

Can you identify the film represented in each photograph? We've supplied some generous hints, and if you fail to identify at least eleven of the films, you need a brushup course in late-movie watching.

Photo 1
A passionate moment between Amy Jolly and her legionnaire. The director: Josef von Sternberg: The year: 1930. The lady's first American film. The gentleman's twenty-third movie.

Photo 2
Here we have Barbara Stanwyck and Gavin Gordon held prisoner by Chinese soldiers, in a scene from Frank Capra's rather bizarre 1932 melodrama.

Photo 3
This tender romantic drama of 1933 was directed in characteristically lyrical fashion by Frank Borzage. It was Loretta Young's thirty-eighth film and the seventeenth for Spencer Tracy.

Photo 4
A difficult film to guess, we admit. Here we see Boris Karloff threatening Myrna Loy (curiously named **Fah Lo See**) and Charles Starrett. An MGM movie, released in 1932.

Photo 5
The director of this film remade it in 1950 as *Riding High.* At right Warner Baxter and Myrna Loy are expressing concern for their ill horse. The year is 1934.

Photos 6 and 7
Here are two photos from films made sixteen years apart. Above: one of the screen's best comedies of the thirties. Below: its extremely pallid remake. Name the two films.

Photo 8
In this tense scene: Ann Sheridan, Frank McHugh, James Cagney, and Anthony Quinn. Cagney is a prize fighter coming on hard times, and Sheridan is his ambitious girlfriend. (This 1940 movie had director Elia Kazan in a featured role.)

Photo 9
Cagney again, this time in 1939 as a reporter framed into prison by the mob. They have knocked him unconscious, poured alcohol all over his car, and sent him careening into a fatal accident. The movie?

Photo 10
One of Alfred Hitchcock's few comedies was this 1941 film with Carole Lombard and Robert Montgomery. It wasn't entirely successful, but it had the charm and skill of the two leading players to sustain it.

Photo 11
These three lovely ladies are readily identifiable as Hedy Lamarr, Judy Garland and Lana Turner. They were appearing in a lavish 1941 musical, along with James Stewart. (Side question: what was the only other film in which Judy Garland and Lana Turner appeared together?)

Photo 12
No, this is not a gathering at a librarians' convention. It is the confrontation scene from a famous 1935 horror film. The lady with the unusual hairdo is Elsa Lanchester.

Photo 13
Here are Bette Davis and Paul Muni, two of the movies' great stars, in one of their lesser-known films, released early in 1935. He plays a Mexican-American lawyer, and she is the promiscuous woman with whom he becomes dangerously involved. (Ida Lupino played the role in a partial remake, *They Drive by Night.*)

Photo 14
This 1946 emotional drama was first made in 1920 under Frank Borzage's direction. Oscar Levant, Joan Crawford, and John Garfield make up the tense trio. This version was directed by Jean Negulesco.

Photo 15

Shoeless Judy Holliday has an altercation with a man in the park in this 1954 release. Taking her photograph is Jack Lemmon in his movie debut. The name of the movie?

(Answers on page 187)

Photo 16

A tender moment from the 1953 film version of a successful play, with Julie Harris, Ethel Waters, and Brandon de Wilde in their original roles.

DO IT AGAIN

Many of the screen's best comedies of the thirties and forties were re-made in later years, frequently as musicals. In each case, match the original film at the left with its remade version at the right.

The Major and the Minor	*Masquerade in Mexico*
The Shop Around the Corner	*How to Marry a Millionaire*
Love Is News	*The Girl Most Likely*
Swing High, Swing Low	*Three for the Show*
Lady For A Day	*About Face*
Nothing Sacred	*Everybody Does It*
It Happened One Night	*That Wonderful Urge*
My Favorite Wife	*Emergency Wedding*
Tom, Dick, and Harry	*I'd Rather Be Rich*
The Philadelphia Story	*Silk Stockings*
Wife, Husband, and Friend	*Walk, Don't Run*
Too Many Husbands	*The Toy Tiger*
True Confession	*You're Never Too Young*
The Greeks Had a Word for It	*The Birds and the Bees*
It Started With Eve	*She's Working Her Way Through College*
Midnight	*When My Baby Smiles at Me*
Bachelor Mother	*High Society*
Mad About Music	*Move Over, Darling*
Ninotchka	*In the Good Old Summertime*
Brother Rat	*Cross My Heart*
The Lady Eve	*Easy to Wed*
You Belong To Me	*You Can't Run Away from It*
The More the Merrier	*Bundle of Joy*
The Male Animal	*A Pocketful of Miracles*
Libeled Lady	*Living It Up*

(Answers on page 188)

THE MALE ANIMAL (1942). With Henry Fonda, Olivia de Havilland and Jack Carson.

THE BARROOM BRAWL:

Notes on Visual Clichés in the Movies

By Robert F. Moss

Swapping old movie clichés has long been a favorite parlor game of film buffs. With seasoned players, the endearingly hackneyed lines may racket back and forth as smoothly as when they were first (or last) delivered on the screen. But lost in the esoteric pleasures of antique dialogue, how many film enthusiasts remember that the camera itself has been as fertile a source of clichés as any writer's pen? With their blood-red sunsets and sunrises, their light flickering through trees in a forest, their figures silhouetted on a hill, the movies have made the visual cliché as much a reality as its verbal cousin. Though often abetted by the scenario, it remains a sovereign entity, a thing unto itself.

In Hollywood the visual cliché has always been particularly at home on the range. The rigid formula of most Westerns—especially before the advent of "adult Westerns"—made it inevitable that the eye would be treated to as many familiar patterns as the ear. Tumbleweeds billowing down empty streets in a ghost town, murderous Indians circling a covered wagon (or, more recently, murderous whites circling the Indians), the town marshal coolly striking a match against a post and lighting a long, thin cigar—these are a few of the old friends that greet the moviegoer in a horse opera. Naturally the most venerable ones are apt to turn up in the key settings of the genre—the saloon, for instance. The population of a Hollywood saloon is always a nondescript bunch of cowboys in gray hats and baggy clothes, slouching dissolutely over their drinks or a hand of cards, totally at ease. All this ends when Johnny Ringo or the Laramie Kid pushes through the swinging doors, casting a spell of silence that no magician could surpass, or causing everyone to leap beneath the tables in fright. The behavior of the secondary villains who lurk somewhere in the saloon is

78

also predictable. Generally employed by the saloon owner —whose dapper Eastern clothes and well-trimmed moustache stamp him unmistakably as the head villain— these thugs exist solely to die ignoble deaths in face-to-face shoot-outs with Ringo or Laramie.

His invincibility in a fair fight having been established, the hero is then considered vulnerable only to ambush, which is attempted—unsuccessfully—from behind two large boulders when he makes a trip to somebody's ranch. Failing at this, the villains wait for the final confrontation in the saloon before resorting to the classic ambush attempt: a lone man with a rifle in the balcony. Detected and outsniped by the hero, the would-be assassin finds himself contemplating a small red hole in his chest. After a second of frozen shock, his last function is to plunge over the railing, describing a smooth downward arc and perhaps demolishing the roulette table as he lands.

If the Western has a single most beloved visual cliché, it is probably the barroom brawl. Like pie-throwing in slapstick comedy, the saloon slugfest usually begins small —tempers heat up, a quarrel develops, a punch is thrown and soon a wild free-for-all, including every available extra, is under way. Judicious close-ups keep us posted on the status of the principals, while alternating long shots serve to remind us not to lose the forest for the trees: this is a group effort, an honest-to-God riot. In the course of the fight, enough tables and chairs are smashed to furnish firewood for most of New England. A mandatory dash of comedy is added when the bartender, very much a non-combatant in these fracases, emerges from behind the bar, where he is in hiding, just long enough to bring a whiskey bottle down on some cowboy's head.

So indisputably a classic is the barroom melee, it can be looked on as practically a grand archetype of *all* visual clichés. There are certainly none that surpass it in splendid, unfading triteness; it is as if a popcorn box should be set in orbit above our planet, there to revolve forever, fixed and eternal.

We cannot leave the subject of visual clichés in the Wild West without a tip of the ten-gallon hat to Roy Rogers, who may be responsible for an amazingly sturdy sequence that he was one of the first to use. In it, Roy finds a small shack in which three members of the gang (one of whom *must* be called Blackie) are hiding out after robbing the stage. Roy intrudes abruptly. What follows is a fistfight that, in its total fidelity to ritualistic detail, compares favorably to Easter mass at the Vatican. One bad guy is immediately knocked unconscious, and

A typical gangland activity

Roy then contends with the little ups and downs of fighting two men at once. He has just completed this arduous process—without ever once using the dirty tricks his antagonists use against him—when the first baddie groggily revives. He now knows better than to meet Roy straight-on and, just as his cohorts have gone down for the count, he crashes a heavy wooden chair over Roy's head (from *behind* naturally), leaving him senseless. In this way, the plot can move along without questioning Roy's virility by suggesting that three-to-one odds are too much for him.

Visual clichés also abound in gangster films. On the strength of movies like *Little Caesar, Scarface, The Enforcer, New York Confidential* and numberless others of the same ilk, it is clear that two iron laws must be obeyed if one is to survive in the underworld: (1) never cross Mr. Big and (2) never say, "If it's all the same to you, boss, I think I'll just take my cut and get out now." In either instance, the offender has just guaranteed himself a quick trip to the morgue. His fate will come in the form of one of two distinguished visual clichés. Either a pair of tough-looking thugs in the back of the room, getting the nod from Mr. Big, will follow the marked man out when he leaves, or the camera will "discover" Mr. Big's hand gliding quietly to a revolver in his desk drawer.

Since the earliest days of talking films, the hired killer has occupied an honored place in gangster movies. Gradually, standardized guidelines for his characterization have evolved. Whatever else he may be, he is automatically *not* what you expect, not your ordinary garden-variety type of killer. Awakened in his tastefully designed apartment, the hit man in *Get Carter* seems courteous and civil in making the arrangements for Michael Caine's assassination. His counterpart in *Point Blank* even smokes a pipe. This gentility does not diminish his professionalism in the least, as we see in another obligatory close-up: expertly, he screws in his telescopic lens just before the kill.

In the gangster genre, different rules—and clichés—apply to the boss himself. Robert Warshow, in his well-known essay "The Gangster as Tragic Hero," observes: "In the opening scene of *Scarface*, we are shown a successful man; we know he is successful because he has just given a party of opulent proportions and because he is called Big Louie. Through some monstrous lack of caution, he permits himself to be alone for a few moments. We understand from this immediately that he is about to be killed. No convention of the gangster film is more strongly established than this: it is dangerous to be alone." Warshow might have added that any Mafia chieftain who puts on a recording of an operatic aria is inviting a hail of gunfire. Then the camera may choose to coyly avoid his corpse in order to concentrate on the record

revolving endlessly in its last groove. The device reached perfection in *Al Capone*, where a character departs from this vale of tears to the strains of *"M'appari"* (*Martha*), with machine-gun accompaniment.

It's only a short ride in a black limousine from gangland to the world of the private eye; indeed, they sometimes occupy the same neighborhood. A movie detective's investigation of an apparently amateur crime often leads, ultimately, to the professionals of the underworld, as in *The Big Sleep* and *Marlowe*. In such cases, the detective's congenital nosiness is apt to result in a visual cliché that any movie buff would recognize instantly, even if it were ruthlessly stripped of its context: a shot of the surveillance man that the gang has stationed in a doorway across the street from the detective's apartment. Although the camera discloses all the telltale signs—the man's heavy overcoat, his hoody appearance, his tendency to stand all day and all night in the same doorway staring up at the same apartment—only the detective (and the audience) instantly grasp their full significance.

Later the private eye's curiosity becomes something of an occupational hazard when he is advised to "stay off the case." The efforts of his enemies to make this advice as persuasive as possible are the source of yet another golden moment in cinematic ritual: lured into an alley, the hero is savagely beaten by two of Mr. Big's men (with the introduction of karate in the sixties, three or four were required). In what is probably the most famous scene of this kind, from *The Big Sleep*, Humphrey Bogart sustains a beating at the hands of two of "Eddie Mars' boys," while Elisha Cook, Jr., looks on. This, like most kindred efforts from the thirties and forties, looks as stylized today as a Japanese Noh drama. It is the "biff-pow" approach to violence. Despite the grunts and groans, it all looks as harmless as slapstick in contrast to, say, *Performance* or *The Laughing Policeman*, where the mandatory visual elements are a kick in the groin and lots of blood.

At one end, the detective film abuts the gangster melodrama; at the other, the murder story. These two overlapping genres share a claim to another of the camera's favorite images—a murder victim-to-be, photographed in stark close-up, as the killer moves in on him. The terrified expression on his face may be accompanied by a simple, gasped comment like "No! No!" or, if he is on more intimate terms with his assailant, "You!!" Requiring only such fragments of dialogue, this much-essayed sequence, almost indispensable to its genre, is primarily visual in nature. In this connection, a special award must go to Tom Conway in *The Cat People*. Playing a psychiatrist who is attacked suddenly by one of his patients, who inconveniently turns out to be a cat woman, Conway is sufficiently swift and resourceful to draw his

A busy monster's laboratory

sword cane to defend himself—although, unfortunately, it proves unequal to the task.

Other possible accoutrements of the murder mystery are: an old Gothic mansion, sliding panels, suits of armor and portraits with roving eyes. But here, however, we are blurring over into another genre—the horror story. Let us dissolve, then, to tales of the supernatural, in which a brooding castle of medieval contours conceals the inhuman experiments of a mad doctor or the nocturnal rounds of a vampire clan. There is no region of filmdom to which the visual cliché has proved more indigenous than Transylvania and Carpathia. The ominous carriage ride that brings an innocent, unsuspecting protagonist— say, Jonathan Harker in *Dracula*—to the castle has taken its place in the great collective unconscious of moviegoers everywhere. Alongside it must be placed the massive door that creaks open autonomously to admit the foolhardy guest; the deaf-mute who "welcomes" him within and guides him to the master; the laboratory, with its vast turbulence of bubbling vats, fizzing tubes and throbbing electrodes; the diaphanously dressed maidens who take midnight strolls at the evil bidding of the villain; the flashes of lightning that illuminate the eerie goings-on during those inopportune moments when the candles have blown out; the primitive but vivid expressions of rage and distress registered on the faces of man-made monsters.

Indeed, the crop of cinematic memorabilia that is avail-

able in the horror movie equals or exceeds that of any other genre. There is something in the nature of horror films that seems to predispose them toward the visual rather than the verbal. Perhaps it is the relatively high degree of subhuman characters, with their constitutionally inarticulate manner. It is not hard to understand why dwarfs, deaf-mutes, hunchbacks and monsters should find facial expressions superior to language and actions preferable to words. Occasionally a mad scientist, falling prey to pedantic impulses, may prove verbose in explaining his process for manufacturing tentacled mutants or little green men, but his grotesque creations can be counted on to forswear all verbiage in favor of a bellow and a crushing blow to someone's skull. With the possible exception of Bela Lugosi's characters—who often seem intent on talking their victims to death—most vampires do not waste their twelve hours of freedom with much gum-beating. During Christopher Lee's reign as the Hammer Studios' Dracula, he was especially successful in increasing the ratio of blood-sucking to dialogue. In *Dracula, Prince of Darkness*, he doesn't even bother to introduce himself (not even so much as a "Good evening, I am Count Dracula") before springing at somebody's throat.

If horror movies are singularly rich in great visual clichés, other genres are just as singularly poor. War films, for instance, have more than their share of immortal lines ("Somebody's got to get that Jap ammunition dump"), but there are very few purely cinematic sequences that can be regarded as chips off an archetypal pattern. Musicals are equally unmemorable in this respect. Apart from the bulging production numbers of Busby Berkeley, renowned for their aerial view of two or three miles of carefully patterned and synchronized chorines, musicals are not where the collector of visual clichés should look. Some case could be made for the rocking trains and narrow corridors of espionage films—and for the sinister man behind the newspaper who awaits the hero at airports and in hotel lobbies—but otherwise the genre is rather barren of visual conventions.

At the same time, some praise must be reserved for those scenes which have won their immortality outside the confines of any particular genre. For example, except for more contemporary movies, any film with a New York setting is apt to be full of characters who, when it comes to finding a parking space, have their own private radar system. In the most crowded sections of Manhattan, these unerring marksmen wheel in and out of their predestined spots. Another sight that any true movie fan should be able to summon out of his memory bank is a film character jumping into someone else's car and somehow starting the engine at once.

Any film of the thirties or forties with a big-city setting may also include what can be termed the "swank nightclub scene." There is never much variety in the physical properties of this scene: the nightclub is about the size of a small Balkan republic, the decor consists of wall-to-wall elegance and the hundreds of tables are filled with swells in evening dress. A singer in glimmering satin performs a song (usually in a husky voice) that no one else has ever heard before or will ever hear again. Then the protagonists—always a man and a woman—applaud politely and begin a conversation. A waiter may or may not show up to take their orders; it really doesn't matter because the food seldom comes and even if it does, not a bit of it is consumed. Instead, the dialogue evolves in such a way (through an argument, a revelation, a resolution that must be followed up immediately) as to effect the couple's departure soon after their arrival. Before leaving, the man discharges any ethical or legal obligations by casually tossing some money on the table—without bothering to count it.

The imprint that most visual clichés have left is, by definition, the result of repetition. Hence it is difficult to find a Platonic form for any of them or to assign credit to any single individual. No one seems to have "invented" the shadow of a killer looming over his victim, though it was used as early as 1920 in Murnau's *Nosferatu*. Rather, such effects grew organically, an expression of collective *kitsch*. In one case, however, we can point to a seminal force: Slavko Vorkapich, one of the great names of movie history (who also, incidentally, happens to have a *great name*).

In Hollywood since the twenties (he was born in Yugoslavia), Vorkapich is an original film theorist whose special skills at developing montage sequences have obscured his reputation as a scholar. (Among his most celebrated credits are the revolution in *Viva Villa* and the famine and exodus in *The Good Earth*.) He is famous as the originator of the "Vorkapich effect," usually a form of montage that telescopes some momentous event which is crucial to the story. For instance, a battle scene in *The Firefly* is collapsed into a few quick shots of storm clouds, clashing swords, falling bodies.

Unfortunately, his innovative techniques have become so trite through endless repetition that, whatever else he may have accomplished, he must also be regarded as the father of many of the screen's noblest visual clichés. Among his illustrious progeny are pages flying off a calendar to signify passage of time, interlocked snatches of song to capsulize a musical career, and churning train wheels to indicate a character's movement from one city to another. The song device is a standby in nearly every musical biography and the train wheels, interestingly enough, were used by Robert Florey, Vorkapich's old colleague, in Chaplin's *Monsieur Verdoux*. Vorkapich has even seen his name converted to a verb—by humorist S. J. Perelman in a mock camera direction: "Vorkapich around the room to Dimitri's brother-officers as they register consternation at the news."

Vorkapich is as good a conclusion as any to these cursory notes, the merest prologue to a subject that is sadly underexplored at the moment. From the most frivolous trivia sessions to the most sober scholarship, the visual cliché offers rich and alluring possibilities. Its "mute eloquence" must no longer go ignored. With that thought, then, let us fade away, leaving only the overturned chair by the dusty table, the curtains flapping futilely by the window, and the screen door swinging slowly backward and forward in the cold Western wind.

FOREIGN MATTER

Each of the following refers directly or indirectly to a renowned foreign film. Name the film for four points each. (A foreign film "maven" should score at least 80 points.)

1. "Nature all looks alike. Frontiers are an invention of man."
2. A clock without hands. A man without a face. An old man confronting his own corpse.
3. A twenty-minute sequence without dialogue or background music was the highlight of this film.
4. The cast of characters: The Man, the Woman, the Bandit, the Firewood Dealer, the Priest, the Commoner, the Medium, and the Police.
5. A beach at Ostia. Dawn. A huge one-eyed fish. A party of revelers.
6. Police officer: "Did anyone witness the incident?" Antonio: "People saw it, sure, but nobody cared."
7. An old lady in a tiny button shop becomes the victim of her assistant's fear and indifference.
8. A drunk black American soldier is robbed of his boots by an Italian urchin.
9. Lola-Lola: "You've come back. They always do."
10. A troubled boy is questioned by a psychiatrist. On screen we only see the face of the boy.
11. What happened in an Austrian hunting lodge on the evening of January 30, 1889?
12. A feudal warlord, scheming to kill the husband of the woman he lusts after, murders the woman by mistake.
13. A feature of this celebrated French film was the detailed reproduction of the legendary nineteenth-century Boulevard of Crime in Paris, where theatres and music halls showed bloody melodramas and freak shows.
14. Don Pietro, a gentle priest, is shot to death when he refuses to divulge information to the Germans.
15. A dying old man sits on a playground swing in the falling snow and rocks back and forth.
16. Zampano, Gelsomina, and Matto the Fool.
17. An anguished murderer screams "I can't help myself!"
18. Where is Anna? Has she committed suicide? Did she find her way back to the mainland? Is she playing a willful game with her lover?
19. On a deserted beach, a knight plays a chess game with Death.
20. In the middle of gunfire and carnage, a baby carriage rolls down a flight of stairs.

21. A nitwit bachelor has a disastrous experience with a collapsible boat.
22. Fernando, passionately attracted to the young Angela, plots to force his wife Rosalia into infidelity so that he can shoot her under the law.
23. A little boy places a girl's rosary beads in an owl's nest and says bitterly, "Keep it a hundred years!"
24. Film director Guido watches the fat whore, La Seraghina, dancing wantonly on the beach.
25. The director: Vittorio De Sica. The scriptwriter: Cesare Zavattini. The principal players: Rinaldo Smordoni and Franco Interlenghi.

(Answers on page 188)

TO THE LADIES

Here are twenty-five women characters in movies, each supplied with an appropriate hint as to the film in which she figured importantly. For four points each name the film and the actress who played the role. (You should score at least 84 points to experience the movie buff's glow of satisfaction.)

1. Sadie Burke ("Win With Willie!")
2. Esther Smith (sisters Tootie, Agnes and Rose)
3. Alicia Huberman (the key to the wine cellar)
4. Pearl Chavez (a fatal shoot-out with Lewt McCanles)
5. Irene Bullock (scavenger hunt for a forgotten man)
6. Terry Randall ("The calla lilies are in bloom again.")
7. Doris Attinger ("After you shot him, how did you feel then?" "Hungry.")
8. Veta Louise Simmons (an alcoholic brother named Elwood)
9. Barbara Graham (doomed lady)
10. Charlotte Inwood ("the Laziest Gal in Town")
11. Amanda Farrow (boss lady)
12. Carlotta Vance ("My dear, you have nothing to worry about.")
13. Arabella Rittenhouse ("You're the most beautiful woman I've ever seen, which doesn't say much for you.")
14. Karen Holmes (Warden's woman)
15. Isabella Linton (Niven's sister)
16. Liza Elliot ("She *would* make up her mind.")
17. Brigid O'Shaughnessy ("You're good. You're very good.")
18. Nina Yakushova ("Fewer but better Russians")
19. Erika Von Schleutow ("Want to buy some illusions?")
20. Sugarpuss O'Shea (a modern-day Snow White)
21. Lucy Warriner (a rendition of "Gone With the Wind")
22. Catherine Sloper (no bride for Morris Townsend)
23. Leslie Benedict (wife to Bick)
24. Tess Harding (Mrs. Sam Craig)
25. Nettie Cleary ("Both Sides Now")

(*Answers on page 188*)

GENTLEMEN OF THE MOVIES

In our quiz *To the Ladies*, we asked you to identify twenty-five women characters in movies and supplied each character with an appropriate hint as to the film in which she figured importantly. Here is a quiz giving equal time to the men. Name the film and the actor who played the role, for four points each.

1. Will Kane ("What will I do if you leave me?")
2. Tony Camonte (sister Cesca, pal Guido)
3. Rocky Sullivan (idol of the "Kids")
4. Sir Wilfrid Robarts (no cigars allowed)
5. Colonel "Bat" Guano ("some kind of prevert")
6. Sid Sorokin (Babe's guy)
7. Freddie Clegg (butterflies and Miranda)
8. Oscar Jaffe ("If there is any justice in the world, Mildred Plotker, you'll end up where you belong— in a burlesque house!")
9. Fast Eddie Felson ("I'm the best there is")
10. Egbert Floud (wife Effie)
11. Adam Lemp (father to Anne, Emma, Kay, and Thea)
12. Jonathan Shields (loved and loathed by Georgia)
13. Uncle Charlie (the "Merry Widow" waltz)
14. Sidney Falco (lackey to J. J. Hunsecker)
15. Alexander Dyle, or Adam Canfield, or Peter Joshua, or Bryan Cruikshank (Paris, Mancini, and a girl named Reggie)
16. Major Pollock (a poignant friendship with Sybil Railton-Bell)
17. Howard Bevans (reluctant bridegroom for Rosemary)
18. Shelby Carpenter (other characters: Mark McPherson, Ann Treadwell)
19. Nick Donati (sister Marie, mistress Fluff)
20. Jonathan Wilk (a plea for Jud and Artie)
21. Atticus Finch (son Jem, daughter Scout)
22. Osgood Fielding III (Daphne's beau)
23. Norval Jones (a husband for Trudy Kockenlocker)
24. Gay Langland ("Just head for that big star. It will take us home.")
25. Gregory Anton (Mr. Manningham on the stage)

(*Answers on page 188*)

MURDER AND MAYHEM

We live in violent times, but then the movies have always shown a penchant for violent themes, with an emphasis on homicide. Below we have twenty imaginary headlines involving the plots of films in which murder or other crimes largely figured. Name the films for five points each. (The photos shown here are clues to several of the answers but we're not telling to which questions!)

1. Body Discovered in Chest by Professor. Two Students Seized.
2. Motel Owner Held in Brutal Murders. Psychiatric Tests Ordered.
3. Woman Companion Trapped Into Confessing Employer's Murder. Asks Retarded Sisters Be Institutionalized.
4. Hidden Ex-Nazi Leader Uncovered in New England Town. Dies in Bizarre Encounter with Town Clock.
5. Homicidal Killer Shot By His Distraught Mother. Mute Servant Girl Rescued.
6. Murder in the Musical World: Noted Pianist Kills Famed Composer.
7. English Country Estate Destroyed By Fire. Housekeeper Perishes in Mysterious Circumstances.
8. Ex-Soldier Arrested For Murder After Police Investigation. Bigotry Seen As Motive.
9. Dateline Malaya. Woman Found Stabbed on Plantation. Was Recently Acquitted in Murder Trial.
10. Blind Woman Routs Assailants in Her Apartment. Mysterious Doll Thought to Be Involved.
11. Wealthy Woman Invalid Found Murdered. Husband Questioned. Police Suggest She May Have Been Seeking Telephone Help.
12. Trapped Killer Dies When Oil Tank Explodes.
13. Terror in the Sky: Woman Lands Plane Safely By Herself—with Three Dead Men Aboard (Husband and Two Pilots Reported Killed in Gun Duel)
14. Barbaric Murder Stuns City. Crippled Elderly Woman Is Thrown Down Stairs in Wheelchair.
15. Playwright-Heiress Claims Husband Homicidal. He and Girlfriend Killed in Car Crash.
16. Leading Publisher Exposed as Murderer By Editor. Killed in Fall Down Elevator Shaft.
17. Ex-Film Star Held in Murder of Writer. Sordid Relationship Hinted.
18. Killer Trapped in Desert Diner. Shoots Man Before Being Killed By Police.
19. Woman Escapes From Vicious Thugs. Trapped in Home Elevator For Days.
20. Man Exposes Town's Complicity in Old Murder. Shoot-Out Leaves Several Dead.

(Answers on page 189)

PHANTOMS OF THE MOVIES

By Curtis F. Brown

Day after day, night after night, month after month, year after year —the same marvelous movies show up on television with maddening frequency, and the same old superstars play out the same wonderful stories, over and over again.

For most of us movie buffs, it's hard to resist watching, no matter how many times we've seen them. There are always two or three lines, or plot and casting details to check out.

But if you happen to be tired of seeing Gable and Colbert spar and spat, if you're weary of watching Judith Anderson drive Joan Fontaine bonkers, if you've thrilled to Jimmy Stewart setting Washington on its ear once too often, and if you've seen Bogart give up Bergman for the umpteenth time, then you have a galloping case of *Rerepeatitis tele-visionus*.

The following little-known movies are offered as a refreshing change from the usual round of first-rate entertainment. Though the titles and casts—maybe even the plots—have a familiar ring, you haven't seen these movies in the theatre. And you won't, alas, ever see them on television. They're merely Movies That Might Have Been (and, probably Just As Well Weren't), described in the typical style of your favorite television guide.

6:15 (11) *Vladivostok Express* (1941). Russian concert violinist and American stevedore meet on train, conspire to topple dictatorship. Anna Sten, Randolph Scott, Philip Dorn, Albert Basserman.

3:15 (10) *Daffodils for Daphne* (1937). Off-beat comedy centers on ghost of florist's murdered wife who sets trap for suspect in department store. Wendy Barrie, Edmund Lowe, Alan Mowbray, Jessie Ralph.

11:45 (8) *Luck of the O'Reillys* (1938). Fugitive jewel thieves seek anonymity and a new start in quiet New England village. Akim Tamiroff, Lupe Velez, Mischa Auer.

2:00 (9) *Constraint* (1935). Navy pilot's career is threatened when he falls for speed typist with shady past. Edward Arnold, Helen Vinson, ZaSu Pitts, Porter Hall.

1:00 (7) *You Take the Cake* (1938). Spinster sisters spat when both enter baked goods contest at county fair. Gale Sondergaard, Spring Byington.

11:00 (9) *Backwater Boogie-Woogie* (1942). Mysterious stranger robs Alabama bank to aid stranded sister act. Andrews Sisters, Robert Paige, Constance Moore, Walter Catlett.

1:00 (12) *Shadow Over Soho* (1936). Wealthy London dentist flees from sinister hygienist. Pre-*Rebecca*

Hitchcock and still suspenseful. Nova Pilbeam, Roger Livesy, Googie Withers, Naunton Wayne.

11:15 (8) *Give Me a Tom-Tom Beat* (1940). Congo uprising forces down-at-heels family to resettle. Gloria Jean, Peter Lind Hayes, Jane Frazee, Ethel Griffies.

6:15 (11) *How's About It* (1941). Hilarious complications ensue when winners of a weekend trip to Duluth find themselves in Akron instead. Stephanie Bachelor, Kirby Grant, Henry Stephenson, Almira Sessions.

9:00 (3) *Lassie's No Lady* (1945). Sudden change in Lassie's status disrupts family's vacation plans. Edmund Gwenn, Donna Corcoran, Frances Rafferty, Selena Royle.

1:15 (2) *Mott Street After Midnight* (1941). Blind society doctor helps best friend's ex-wife elude Oriental extortion ring. Lee Bowman, Patsy Kelly, Warren Hymer, Keye Luke.

4:15 (10) *Ride Him, Omar!* (1942). Egyptian jockey twists ankle to avoid throwing race. Sabu, Evelyn Keyes, Monty Woolley, Willie Best.

3:25 (6) *Land Sakes* (1937). Case of mistaken identity involves veteran dance team in Oklahoma land rush. Esther Dale, C. Aubrey Smith, Scotty Beckett, Florence Bates.

3:10 (11) *Smile When You're Happy* (1937). Smart kid from city slums wins country cousins' gratitude when he teaches them crop rotation. Bobby Breen, Cora Sue Collins, Isobel Elsom, Henry Kolker.

11:00 (9) *Burn, My Heart!* (1940). Embittered beauty contest loser rushes into marriage with hard-drinking, disbarred attorney. Beverly Roberts, Edward Norris, Victor Jory.

9:00 (10) *Who Is Gus Farmer?* (1938). Amnesia victim finds himself a juror in fiancée's murder trial. Gloria Henry, William Henry, Henry O'Neill, Henry Armetta.

2:00 (4) *Tijuana Holiday* (1942). Color musical. Girl on Mexican vacation has problems with men and drinking water. Carole Landis, Cesar Romero, Chris-Pin Martin, Sir Cedric Hardwicke.

1:15 (8) *River of Tears* (1938). Sacrificing mother is distraught to discover son is embalmer—at age twelve. Kay Francis, Dickie Moore, Rondo Hatton, Emma Dunn.

3:00 (11) *Eat Your Heart Out* (1940). Cannibal invades Louisiana mansion in swamps, causing hilarious confusion. Bud Abbott, Lou Costello, Una Merkel, Gladys Cooper.

LAND SAKES (1937). With C. Aubrey Smith and Florence Bates

LUCK OF THE O'REILLYS (1938). With Akim Tamiroff and Lupe Velez

DISNEY AND HIS FRIENDS

This quiz celebrates the undisputed master of popular family entertainment: Walt Disney. Each question centers on one of his films and is worth four points.

1. In which movie was Timothy Q. Mouse a prominent character?

2. Name the narrator and the musical conductor of *Fantasia*.

3. This is a perfectly true statement: the son of the singer whose voice was used for the prince in *Snow White and the Seven Dwarfs* later portrayed a child murderer. Name the singer and his son.

4. "I give myself very good advice (but I very seldom follow it)" is the musical reflection of which Disney heroine?

5. Pecos Bill was a rip-roaring Disney Western hero in one of the segments of which film: *Fun and Fancy Free, Melody Time,* or *Make Mine Music?*

6. A terrifying moment in *Pinocchio* comes when the little hero's companion-in-trouble turns into a donkey. What is this character's name?

7. A fantastic basketball game, with players leaping over the heads of their opponents, was the highlight of which Disney movie?

8. *Mary Poppins* marked the last appearance of a well-loved character actress. She had no lines but was rather touching as a ragged old derelict who feeds the birds. What was her name?

9. The same actress gave her voice to *Alice in Wonderland* and to Wendy in *Peter Pan.* Was she Mary Costa, Ilene Woods, or Kathryn Beaumont?

10. Which Disney film included the songs "Twitterpated"

A scene from ALICE IN WONDERLAND (1951). © Walt Disney Productions

A scene from SLEEPING BEAUTY (1959). © Walt Disney Productions

and "Let's Sing a Gay Little Spring Song"?

11. In Disney movies, this actress has played characters named Sharon McKendrick, Mary Grant, Nancy Carey, Nikki Ferris, and Patti Randall. Her name?

12. In Disney's 1960 version of Robert Louis Stevenson's *Kidnapped,* who played the role of David Balfour, performed by Freddie Bartholomew in Fox's 1938 version?

13. Donald Duck and Joe Carioca are two of Disney's *Three Caballeros,* in that 1945 mixture of animation and live action. Name the third caballero.

14. Who played the father in Disney's 1960 version of *Swiss Family Robinson*?

15. "Stick-to-it-ivity" is a typical Disney song title from which of the following movies: *So Dear to My Heart, Song of the South,* or *Summer Magic*?

16. In *Make Mine Music,* name the comedian whose voice was featured in "Casey at the Bat."

17. Name the film which used the voices of Phil Harris, Sebastian Cabot, George Sanders, Sterling Holloway, and Louis Prima.

18. This veteran performer was virtually a member of Disney's later stock company, with featured roles in *The Absent-Minded Professor, Babes in Toyland, Son of*

Flubber, Mary Poppins, Those Calloways, That Darn Cat, and *The Gnome-mobile.* His name?

19. Which of the following is *not* one of Cinderella's friends in the Disney version: Bruno the dog, Lucifer the cat, Jacques the mouse, Flower the skunk?

20. In the 1954 version of Jules Verne's *20,000 Leagues Under the Sea,* was the villainous Captain Nemo played by Peter Finch, Alastair Sim, James Mason, or James Robertson Justice?

21. Flora and Fauna are two of the three good fairies in *Sleeping Beauty.* Who was the third?

22. Model Marjorie Belcher posed for the character of Snow White. Later her name changed when she became part of a popular dance team. Her new name?

23. In Disney's film about the legendary hero Davy Crockett, which of the following actors played Davy's sidekick, George Russell: Edgar Buchanan, Walter Brennan, Buddy Ebsen, or Royal Dano?

24. Who narrated *The Legend of Sleepy Hollow*: Burl Ives, Bing Crosby, or Sterling Holloway?

25. Which of the following was Disney's first feature-length film in the True-Life nature series: *White Wilderness, The Living Desert, The Vanishing Prairie,* or *The African Lion*?

(*Answers on page 189*)

THEM THAR HILLS

Here's a quiz for lovers of Western movies—but beware. We've tossed in some tough questions that should give every "armchair cowboy" something to think about. (Five points for each correct answer, and no partial points, either.)

1. In *Jesse James* (1939), who played the "dirty little coward" who shot and killed James? Was it Brian Donlevy, John Carradine, or Henry Hull?

2. Which of the following movies is *not* a Western? *Pursued* (1947), *Trapped* (1949), *Convicted* (1950), *Branded* (1950)

3. Which of the following movies *is* a Western? *Shoot First* (1953), *Border Incident* (1949), *A Bullet for Joey* (1955), *Gun for a Coward* (1957)

4. Name the two films in which Raymond Massey played fiery abolitionist John Brown.

5. Harry Carey and Harry Carey, Jr. appeared together in only one film. Was it *Three Godfathers, She Wore a Yellow Ribbon*, or *Red River*?

6. In a Western movie sense, what do Walter Huston, Victor Mature, and Kirk Douglas share in common?

7. Even Joan Crawford rode the range on occasion. In 1954, in *Johnny Guitar,* she was the hard-bitten owner of a Western gambling house. Who played her adversary?

8. A 1954 Western drama, *Broken Lance,* with Spencer Tracy and Richard Widmark, was a remake of a 1949 movie in an entirely different setting. It starred Edward

G. Robinson and Richard Conte. Name the film.

9. In *Butch Cassidy and the Sundance Kid,* who played Etta Place, the girl involved with both men?

10. Name any two of the three Western movies made by James Cagney.

11. A 1933 Western called *Riders of Destiny* starred Gabby Hayes, Cecilia Parker (later Andy Hardy's sister), and Al St. John. Who played the male lead?

12. In a Western movie sense, what do Walter Brennan and Paul Newman have in common?

13. One of the most powerful Westerns ever made is *The Ox-Bow Incident* (1943). It concerned a brutal lynching in the Old West. Who played the Mexican victim of the lynching?

14. In *The Virginian* (1929), Gary Cooper reacted to Walter Huston's muttered oath with the famous line, "If you want to call me that, smile." Who played the Cooper and Huston roles in the 1946 remake?

15. *One-Eyed Jacks* was an off-beat 1961 Western with Marlon Brando and Karl Malden in the leading roles. Name the director.

16. In *The Gunfighter* (1950), troubled hero Gregory Peck was gunned down by a young punk played by which of the following actors: Richard Jaeckel, Darryl Hickman, Skip Homeier, or Robert Arthur?

17. *Colorado Territory* was a 1949 Western about an old-time outlaw who makes one last desperate stand. It starred Joel McCrea and Virginia Mayo. The film was a remake of a 1941 melodrama, also directed by Raoul Walsh. Name this film.

18. Errol Flynn appeared in eight Warners Westerns between 1939 and 1950. Name the four movies which included a city in their titles.

19. Randolph Scott starred in innumerable Westerns, mainly in the forties and early fifties. Which of the following actresses did *not* appear as one of his leading ladies? Kay Francis, Joan Bennett, Joanne Dru, Angela Lansbury, Donna Reed.

20. In the 1966 remake of *Stagecoach,* who played the timid whiskey drummer originally played by Donald Meek? And who played the alcoholic doctor originally played by Thomas Mitchell?

(Answers on page 189)

RULE, BRITANNIA!

Here are twenty-five questions revolving about films made in England, featuring many of my favorite players and movies. Score four points for each correct answer—and tally ho!

1. As the mad medium, Madame Arcati, she tried to exorcise the ghost of a deceased wife. Name this wonderful actress and the film in which she did her exorcising.
2. One of the funniest British farces had Alastair Sim playing a headmaster named Wetherby Pond. What was the film?
3. The 1941 film version of George Bernard Shaw's *Major Barbara* boasted a stellar cast. Who played the munitions tycoon, Andrew Undershaft? And who played Major Barbara's fiance, Adolphus Cusins?
4. Making her film debut in *The Private Life of Henry VIII* (1933) as Catherine Howard was Binnie Barnes, Wendy Barrie, Elsa Lanchester, or Kay Walsh?
5. "One is *starved* for Technicolor up there!" From which British movie does this line come?
6. A mine disaster. An Irish fugitive. Zither music. "Where Is Love?" All these phrases evoke major films by a fine British director. His name? And can you name the films evoked?
7. Is the heroine of *Genevieve* (1954) a lovable hunting dog, a flirtatious mermaid, or an antique car?

8. Which Alfred Hitchcock film, made in England, featured a missing finger as an important clue?
9. Jessie Matthews was a popular musical star of the thirties. In which movie did she sing Rodgers and Hart's "Dancing on the Ceiling"?
10. Which of the following actresses played opposite David Niven in *Court-Martial* (1955): Celia Johnson, Margaret Leighton, or Valerie Hobson?
11. In 1938, he gave a wonderful performance in *Pygmalion* as Eliza Doolittle's rowdy father. Twenty-eight years later, in *The Wrong Box*, he was equally wonderful as a tottering old servant. His name?
12. This actor has played Maxwell Frere, Andrew Crocker-Harris, and Ernest Worthing. Name this actor (and, if you can, the films in which he played these roles).
13. The actress with a memorable voice who played Daphne Birnley in *The Man in the White Suit* (1952) was Glynis Johns, Joan Greenwood, or Googie Withers?
14. *The Titfield Thunderbolt* (1953) is a British comedy about an aborted rocket, a commuter train, or a rare, multi-colored bird?

15. In which of the following movies did Dirk Bogarde *not* appear: *The Doctor's Dilemma*, *The Singer Not the Song*, *Encore*, or *Agent 8¾*?

16. Now a popular singer, she was a child actress in British films (*London Town*, 1946, *I Know Where I'm Going*, 1947) and later a pert ingenue in such films as *The Promoter* (1952) and *The Runaway Bus* (1954). Her name?

17. The 1954 comedy, *Man With a Million*, had an American star and was based on a story by a famous American writer. Can you name both?

18. Which of the following films starred Rex Harrison: *The Astonished Heart* (1950), *Last Holiday* (1950), *The Long Dark Hall* (1951), or *Simon and Laura* (1956)?

19. The screenplay for the 1952 film, *Breaking Through the Sound Barrier*, concerning the attempt to move through the air at supersonic speed, was written by which of the following: T. E. B. Clarke, Terence Rattigan, or Eric Ambler?

20. In which movie did Alec Guinness play characters named Young Ascoyne and Lady Agatha?

21. Name the 1939 British film in which C. Aubrey Smith related—over and over again—how he won a crucial battle in the Crimean War.

22. James Thurber's story, "The Catbird Seat," was made into a 1960 comedy with Peter Sellers entitled *The Weaker Sex*, *Only Two Can Play*, or *The Battle of the Sexes*?

23. Probably England's greatest actor, Sir Laurence Olivier has appeared in a number of film versions of Shakespeare's plays. His first, *As You Like It*, was produced in 1936. Who played Rosalind to his Orlando?

24. In *Seven Days to Noon* (1950), who played the disturbed scientist who threatens to blow up London unless atom bombs are outlawed?

25. A fleeting appearance in *The Lavender Hill Mob* (1951) is made by which actress: Hermione Gingold, Audrey Hepburn, or Deborah Kerr?

(*Answers on page 189*)

A CROSSWORD PUZZLE FOR MOVIE BUFFS

By Curtis F. Brown

ACROSS

1 Star of *Hitting a New High, That Girl from Paris,* etc.
5 "——— in the stilly night . . ." (More)
8 *Les Etats* ———
12 *So* ——— *My Love*
13 Subject of 1936 Oscar winner for Best Production
14 *Sunday Dinner* ——— ——— *Soldier*
15 Advice, counsel (archaic)
16 He played opposite 1 Across
18 Opus: Abbr.
19 Move stealthily
21 Poet's contraction
22 Reply: Abbr.
23 Fruit
25 Danced by Astaire-Rogers in *Carefree*
27 Cameron Mitchell role, for short (*Death of a Salesman*)
30 Rural routes: Abbr.
31 Comic in *Panama Hattie, Girl Crazy, Anchors Aweigh,* etc.
34 Co-starred with Bergman, Streisand, e.g.
36 Belonging to Miss Andre
38 Murnau-Flaherty collaboration
39 ——— *Arne's Treasure,* silent directed by Stiller
40 *You Are What You* ———
41 MacMurray-Goddard comedy, for short
43 Actor Bevans
45 ——— *of Love*
47 *To* ——— *With Love*
49 Man of wealth and prominence
53 Military officer (abbr.)

54 ——— *City Revels*
56 Starred as Legendre in *White Zombie*
57 Spicy stew
59 Belonging to actor Heggie
60 Israeli diplomat
61 He was pre-stardom extra in *Pigskin Parade, The Goldwyn Follies, Citizen Kane,* e.g.
62 Military officers (abbr.)
63 Impart

DOWN

1 A Westmore
2 ——— *the Moon*
3 Nest or brood of pheasants
4 *The Big* ———
5 *Turn* ——— *the Moon*
6 Room surfaces
7 Made movie debut in *The Wiser Sex,* opposite Colbert
8 German film company
9 *The Girl Said* ———
10 *Man of* ———, B. MacLane starrer
11 ——— *at Sea*
17 *Keep Your Powder* ———
20 Jacopo ———, composer of early opera
22 *I Was* ——— ——— *War Bride*
24 Comic-strip canine's word
26 Mr. Onassis, to friends
27 Former President, to the press
28 Expression of triumph
29 German director
32 She starred in *The Garment Jungle, The Guns of Navarone,* etc.
33 Concorde, e.g.
35 Karel Capek play
36 Comic in *The Fleet's In, Rainbow Island, Practically Yours,* etc.
37 Small brownish bird
39 Basis for a movie
42 Martin and ——— Johnson, explorer team of *I Married Adventure*
44 Actress Paige
45 Mil. offense
46 Soft drink
48 *The Fallen* ———
50 Mrs. Lyon
51 Oscar-winning role for Rainer
52 ——— *of Angels*
54 Star of *The Ten Commandments, Resurrection, Our Modern Maidens,* etc.
55 Movie that starred 61 Across
58 ———*Rather be Rich*

(Answers on page 190)

MORE MOVIE MATTERS

Gleanings From the Silent Era

Here are some fascinating nuggets of information on the films and film personalities of the silent years:

Before turning to direction in the late twenties, Mervyn LeRoy appeared in a few films. He had small roles in Warners' *Little Johnny Jones* (1923), based on George M. Cohan's play; *Going Up* (1923), from a musical play by Otto Harbach and Louis A. Hirsch, and *Broadway After Dark* (1924), adapted from a play by Owen Davis, with Adolphe Menjou and Norma Shearer in the leads. *Little Johnny Jones* was remade in 1929 under LeRoy's direction, with Eddie Buzzell in the leading role. (A short while later, Buzzell himself turned to direction.) *Going Up* was also remade in 1929 as *The Aviator*, with Edward Everett Horton in the lead.

The 1929 film version of W. Somerset Maugham's *The Letter*, starring the ill-fated Jeanne Eagels, featured Herbert Marshall in the role of Leslie Crosbie's secret lover, Geoffrey Hammond. This role was only briefly visible in the better-known 1940 version starring Bette Davis. (He appears in the brilliant opening scene, shot dead by Mrs. Crosbie.) In the 1940 film, Marshall played the cuckolded husband.

A little-remembered version of Booth Tarkington's *The Magnificent Ambersons* was released by Vitagraph in 1925 under the title *Pampered Youth*. It was directed by David Smith, who had directed a version of *Captain Blood* the year before. George Amberson (who finally gets his comeuppance) was played by Ben Alexander as a boy and Cullen Landis as a young man. The movie won respectable reviews but it was greatly overshadowed by Orson Welles' version, seventeen years later.

Harry Leon Wilson's story, *Ruggles of Red Gap*, received its most famous interpretation in Paramount's 1935 version with Charles Laughton. Earlier versions were filmed in 1918 and 1923. In the 1923 film, Ruggles, the English butler who makes his way in the American West, was played by a thirty-six-year-old actor named Edward Horton. In his fifth film, *Beggar on Horseback* (1925), the billing was changed to Edward Everett Horton.

THE LETTER (1929). With Jeanne Eagels and Herbert Marshall

The veteran comedy team of Joe Weber and Lew Fields appeared in only one film in the silent era: a 1925 version of the 1918 play, *Friendly Enemies*, by Samuel Shipman and Aaron Hoffman. As two German-American fathers with confused loyalties during World War I, they were directed by George Melford, who had guided Rudolph Valentino through *The Sheik* two years earlier. (*Friendly Enemies* was remade in 1942, with Charles Winninger and Charles Ruggles as the battling friends, now torn over World War II.)

Thirties heiress Peggy Hopkins Joyce is remembered by buffs for her appearance in *International House*, that demented farce of 1933, with W. C. Fields and George Burns and Gracie Allen. But she had appeared seven years earlier in a silent film called *The Skyrocket*, based on a novel by Adela St. Johns. Under Marshall Neilan's direction, she played a Hollywood extra who becomes a star but who finally returns to her childhood sweetheart (Owen Moore).

In May 1926, a film introducing Paramount's Junior Stars opened at the Rivoli in New York. Called *Fascinating Youth* and directed by Sam Wood, it featured the screen debuts of sixteen new players. Of the sixteen, only two—Charles "Buddy" Rogers and Thelma Todd—achieved any degree of fame. The same players appeared after the movie in a stage presentation designed by John Murray Anderson.

Among the "explanatory" film titles of the twenties were: *Why Girls Leave Home* (1921), *Why Men Forget* (1922), *Why Women Re-Marry* (1923), *Why Men Leave Home* (1924), *Why Husbands Go Mad* (1924), *Why Women Love* (1925), *Why Girls Go Back Home* (1926), *Why Sailors Go Wrong* (1928), and *Why Women Divorce* (1929).

In 1927 Wallace Beery starred in a freely adapted version of that perennial chestnut, *Casey at the Bat*. As a small-town junkman who is signed to play for the New York Giants, Beery is told: "Pack up your other suit, Big Boy. New York's paging you. You'll forget Tanktown Tillie when you see the Broadway beauties." And who played Tanktown Tillie? None other than ZaSu Pitts.

How are these for titillating titles? *The Sin Flood* (1922), *Her Temporary Husband* (1923), *The Painted Flapper* (1924), *Married Flirts* (1924), *The Price of Pleasure* (1925), *Soft Cushions* (1927), *Ankles Preferred* (1927), and *Powder My Back* (1928).

Many stars in their early silent years found themselves playing all sorts of roles, often improbable in the light of their later screen image. A case in point: the dapper, debonair William Powell, who was featured in scores of silent films before becoming one of the screen's best comedians in the sound era. Very often he was cast as a villain: a Spanish dandy who gets involved in some skulduggery in Cuba (*The Bright Shawl*, 1923); the cowardly stool-pigeon Boldini in *Beau Geste* (1926); Eddie Cantor's nemesis in *Special Delivery* (1927). He often appeared with Bebe Daniels: as a scoundrelly prince who marries heiress Daniels in *Dangerous Money*

OUTCAST (1922). With William Powell and Elsie Ferguson

(1924); as a comic Arabian sheik who is playfully mocked by Daniels in *She's a Sheik* (1927), or as a rogue who is the victim of heroine Daniels' expert swordsmanship in *Señorita* (1927).

Virginia Grey, that tart-tongued salesgirl, waitress, or "other woman" of films from the thirties to the sixties, started her film career in quite a different sort of role: she played Little Eva in a 1927 film version of *Uncle Tom's Cabin*. The *New York Times* review remarked that she was "another gifted and very pretty child," although "she does look to be rather healthy when she is supposed to be ailing." Reportedly the film cost more than $1,500,000 to produce and was in production for nearly two years. (Ms. Grey made two more films in 1928, then, after a few bit roles, became an MGM contract player in 1936.)

UNCLE TOM'S CABIN (1927), with James B. Lowe and Virginia Grey

PRIVATE IZZY MURPHY (1926). George Jessel as Izzy

Lloyd Bacon's 1926 comedy, *Private Izzy Murphy*, was cited by *The New York Times* as the feature film debut of comedian George Jessel. Not so. He had appeared in a small role in a 1919 film called *The Other Man's Wife*, with Stuart Holmes and Evelyn Brent. Incidentally, *Private Izzy Murphy* was hardly notable, but it had one unusual piece of casting. The imposingly named Gustav von Seyffertitz, a strong actor in aristocratic or military roles of a decidedly Prussian bent, here played the heroine's Irish father, named Cohannigan.

Louis Joseph Vance's perennial character Michael Lanyard, better known as "The Lone Wolf," was the hero of many entertaining low-budget melodramas of the thirties and forties, most often with Warren William in the role. But The Lone Wolf, a dashing jewel thief who moved to the side of the law, also appeared in the twenties in a few films. He was played by Jack Holt in *The Lone Wolf* (1924), and by Bert Lytell in *Alias the Lone Wolf* (1927) and *the Lone Wolf's Daughter* (1929). (Incidentally, there is one Lone Wolf movie that is seldom cited with the others. *Cheaters at Play*, a Fox film released in 1932, featured veteran actor Thomas Meighan as Michael Lanyard, with Charlotte Greenwood as the lady whose emeralds are stolen [not by Lanyard].)

The famous stage team of Alfred Lunt and Lynn Fontanne appeared only rarely in films, most notably in their 1931 version of their 1924 Ferenc Molnar play, *The Guardsman*. They did play together in an obscure 1924 movie called *Second Youth*, directed by Albert Parker. Lunt was a department store clerk who falls in love—but not with Ms. Fontanne, who only had a featured role. His co-star was an actress named Mimi Palmeri, whose second and last film this was. Lunt's other films in the twenties were equally undistinguished, but Ms. Fontanne was featured in a movie with interesting credentials: *The Man Who Found Himself* (1925) was adapted from a Booth Tarkington story and directed by Alfred E. Green (already his fourteenth film), and the cast included Thomas Meighan, Virginia Valli, Frank and Ralph Morgan, and Victor Moore.

Contrary to popular belief, Clifton Webb did not make his film debut in *Laura* (1944) as the acidulous columnist, Waldo Lydecker. In the silent years, the dashing actor and dancer appeared with Ina Claire in *Polly With a Past* (1921)—it was Ms. Claire's film debut—in *New Toys* (1925) with Richard Barthelmess, and in *The Heart of a Siren* (1925), with Barbara La Marr.

In the twenties and early thirties, which actor played roles later played by such varied actors as Cary Grant, Ray Milland, Alan Ladd, Robert Redford, Don Ameche, John Boles, Wendell Corey, and Fred Astaire? The answer: stalwart Warner Baxter, who starred in films from the early twenties to the late forties. In 1925 he appeared as the divorced husband in *The Awful Truth*, the role later undertaken by Cary Grant (1937) and Ray Milland (*Let's Do It Again*, 1953). In 1926 he starred as Jay Gatsby in *The Great Gatsby*, recreated by Alan Ladd in 1949 and by Robert Redford in 1974. He was the heroine's ill-fated lover and husband in the 1928 version of *Ramona*, a role played by Don Ameche in 1936. In 1928 he was Harriet Craig's long-suffering husband in *Craig's Wife*, played by John Boles and Wendell Corey in the 1936 and 1950 remakes, respectively. And in 1931, he appeared as Jarvis Pendleton, the millionaire with the winsome ward, in *Daddy Long Legs*. Fred Astaire played Pendleton in the 1955 musical version. However, Warner Baxter's principal fame stems from his role as the harried producer in *42nd Street*. (He delivers the immortal line to Ruby Keeler: "You're going out a youngster—but you've got to come back a star!")

THE GREAT GATSBY (1926). With Neil Hamilton, Lois Wilson, and Warner Baxter

THREE:
THE MOVIE THEATRE—FROM PALACE TO "NABE"

Most movie buffs have cherished memories of the theatres they attended as children—of the special glow they experienced when they realized that a lifelong love affair had begun with those flickering images on the screen.

In this section, writers recall that experience with warmth and affection. I also include my own tribute to one of the greatest of the vanished movie "cathedrals": the Roxy Theatre.

WHERE FANTASY REIGNED:

The Glorious Roxy Theatre

By Ted Sennett

"I'm happy. Take a look at this stupendous theatre. It's the Roxy and
I'm Roxy. I'd rather be Roxy than John D. Rockefeller or Henry Ford."
—Samuel L. Rothafel at the opening ceremonies of the Roxy Theatre.

March 11, 1927. It was indeed a night to remember:
an occasion of breathtaking splendor in which the glitter-
ing, absurd, and unforgettable age of the Movie Palace
reached its zenith. After only ten months and thirteen
days of feverish activity, The Cathedral of the Motion
Picture, otherwise known as the Roxy Theatre, was
finally opening its doors.

This long-awaited event brought out the celebrities in
profusion. New York's jaunty Mayor Jimmy Walker was
present, as were such luminous representatives of Hollywood as Harold Lloyd, Richard Dix, Lois Wilson, and
Mary Brian. The founding father, Samuel Lionel
("Roxy") Rothafel, was present, of course, along with
wife Rosa and daughter Beta. Members of the press were
given gold pencils (inscribed with their names) as lifetime passes. Thousands of visitors moved under the
enormous crystal chandelier and amidst the five-story
columns of *verde* marble. They had come to see an elaborate inaugural stage presentation and, incidentally, a
movie: *The Love of Sunya,* with Gloria Swanson and
John Boles.

The theatre they entered was unquestionably an architectural wonder: the world's largest to date, with over
6,200 seats, all luxuriously upholstered, and arranged
to provide ample room between rows. The auditorium
was described as looking "like a huge hammered bronze
bowl with its deep rich plush and simple but dignified
hangings with little gold and red fringe." Draperies were
designed to provide a two-color effect that would absorb
light. The foyers and lobbies were spectacularly large,
and indeed everything in the theatre could only be described in hyperbole. The theatre boasted the largest
permanent symphony orchestra in existence. It had a
huge Kimball pipe organ, the largest in any theatre in
the world, which was played simultaneously by three
organists on three separate consoles. (The main organ
chamber was sixty feet long, thirteen feet deep, and
eighteen feet high.) There was a permanent choral group
of one hundred voices and a permanent ballet corps of
fifty dancers. Also for the first time in any theatre, there
was a set of twenty-one grand chimes. The theatre's
music library, containing ten thousand numbers and
fifty thousand orchestrations, came partly from Victor
Herbert's library.

The Roxy's opening ceremonies were both awesome
and preposterous. Three organists with names to suit the
occasion—Dezso Von D'Antalffy, Emil Velazco, and
Casimir A. J. Parmentier—played the consoles, followed
by a figure robed as a monk, who read the invocation
from a scroll: "Ye portals, bright, high, and majestic,
open to our gaze the path to wonderland, and show us
the realm where fantasy reigns, where romance, where
adventure flourish. Let every day's toil be forgotten
under thy sheltering roof—O glorious, mighty hall—thy
magic and thy claim unite us all to worship at beauty's
throne. Let there be light." Four conductors led the
orchestra through the night's music: Erno Rapee, Charles
Previn, H. Maurice Jacquet, and Frederick Stahlberg.

The evening's program consisted of a series of lavish
presentations. Following the invocation, there was a
musical staging of the writing of "The Star Spangled
Banner," climaxed by its performance. "A Floral Fantasy," a ballet featuring Maria Gambarelli, was followed
by filmed greetings (seen but not heard) from President
Coolidge, Mayor Walker, Governor Smith, Vice-Presi-
dent Davies, and Thomas Edison. One bizarre moment
had 300 patients at Walter Reed Hospital arranged on
the lawn of the hospital to spell out Roxy's name. There
was another scenic fantasy with amazing effects, called
"A Fantasy of the South," a Roxy Pictorial Review,
which was a newsreel assembled from the best shots of
all the commercial newsreels of the week, and a staging
of the song, "A Russian Lullaby," written by Irving
Berlin especially for the opening. Erno Rapee then con-
ducted the overture to *Carmen,* and a Vitaphone short
with Giovanni Martinelli and Jeanne Gordon singing

The lobby of the Roxy Theatre

arias from *Carmen* (seen and heard, in this case) concluded the program. Following the showing of the film, *The Love of Sunya*, "Roxy" Rothafel made an address, stating, "I'm happy. Take a look at this stupendous theatre. It's the Roxy and I'm Roxy. I'd rather be Roxy than John D. Rockefeller or Henry Ford."

With all the official pronouncements on the opening of "The Cathedral of the Motion Picture," none could match the purple, effusive prose of the lavish 50-page souvenir book prepared by the editors of *The Film Daily* especially for the occasion. Comments on "Roxy" himself by playwright Robert E. Sherwood enthused that "the elaborate structure glows with the warming personality of Samuel L. Rothafel." The Roxy's opening meant that "Roxy is to have his own temple, in which he himself is the supreme high priest, at liberty to conduct services in his own way." Sherwood waxed rhapsodic, calling the theatre "a blending of the finest concepts in engineering, architecture, science, and art. In truth, the humble cocoon has given forth the gorgeous butterfly, resplendent in the exquisite form and color conceived by genius."

An article on "The Romance of the Roxy" by Jack Alicoate was close to hysteria in its praise of the theatre,

Opening night at the Roxy Theatre: March 11, 1927

calling it "a shrine dedicated to the universal language of music . . . a veritable fairyland of novelty, comfort, and convenience . . . a harmonious blending of luxurious draperies clothing an architectural masterpiece . . . the magician's workshop—the home of the genii—the castle of the giants." "When you enter its portals," the article exclaimed, "you step magically from the drab world of confusion and cares into a fairy palace whose presiding genius entertains you royally with all the fine allurements that art, science, and music can offer."

The Roxy Theatre survived this opening event and went on to attract the moviegoing public—through good times and bad—for thirty-three years. However, despite the promise of the ultimate in movie entertainment, the first five years of its existence were hardly auspicious, with the management preferring to concentrate on extravagant stage shows. The first film, *The Love of Sunya*, starred Gloria Swanson as a woman permitted to see into the future, to learn how she would fare as the wife of three different men. The next attraction, *Wolf's Clothing*, with Monte Blue and Patsy Ruth Miller, was indicative of the fare the theatre would offer for its first few years: mostly low-budget comedies and melodramas with "titillating" titles so prevalent at the time: *Ankles Preferred* (Madge Bellamy, Lawrence Gray), *Singed* (Blanche Sweet), *Soft Living* (John Mack Brown), *Not Quite Decent*, *Girls Gone Wild*, and *Pleasure-Crazed*. (The first all-talking feature turned up early in 1929.)

There were only a few distinctive films at the Roxy until 1930. Raoul Walsh's *In Old Arizona* (1929) won Warner Baxter an Academy Award for his performance as the dashing Cisco Kid. Paul Muni made his film debut in *The Valiant* (1929), as a nobly sacrificial convict. One of the "all-star" musical revues popular at the time, *Fox Movietone Follies of 1929*, played the theatre in May of that year. And Will Rogers' first sound film, *They Had to See Paris*, had a single week's run in October. One of the raucous Quirt-Flagg comedies, *The Cockeyed World*, also played the theatre that year.

By the beginning of the new decade, the fare at the Roxy was improving, but not to any marked degree. One curious novelty in early 1930 was the presentation of the first "Grandeur audible picture" from Fox, *Happy Days*, an all-star musical with Janet Gaynor, Will Rogers, Charles Farrell, Warner Baxter, Victor McLaglen, and Edmund Lowe among the many performers. For this production, the theatre expanded its already large screen to a width of forty-two feet and a height of twenty feet. The single Grandeur frame was twice that of the standard film and slightly higher. The sound track was also three times as wide as that of the standard film, presumably resulting in more modulated voices and more natural incidental sounds. Despite the ballyhoo, the Grandeur

process did not catch on.

Other 1930 films at the Roxy included *High Society Blues*, with the popular team of Janet Gaynor and Charles Farrell, and *The King of Jazz*, John Murray Anderson's first contribution to talking films, a lavish Technicolor revue starring Paul Whiteman and his orchestra, John Boles, Laura La Plante, and other Fox stars. (Inevitably, Whiteman played George Gershwin's "Rhapsody in Blue," which, curiously enough, was repeated in the stage presentation, with Gershwin himself at the piano.) *The New Movietone Follies of 1930* was another musical potpourri which featured Marjorie White singing "I'd Love to Be a Talking Picture Queen." A somewhat more prestigious film than usual was Frank Borzage's production of Ferenc Molnar's *Liliom*, with Charles Farrell, Rose Hobart, Lee Tracy, Walter Abel, and Estelle Taylor.

In the next few years, the routine movie fare was punctuated with several surprises. In February 1931, the theatre showed Bela Lugosi in his classic performance of *Dracula*. *The New York Times* called it "the best of the many mystery films" and praised Lugosi for producing the proper bloodcurdling effects, but the movie was followed in only one week by Fox's newest version of *East Lynne*, with Ann Harding. Other highlights of 1931 at the Roxy were Raoul Walsh's *The Yellow Ticket*, with Lionel Barrymore as a wicked baron and Elissa Landi as his innocent prey (the cast included Laurence Olivier, Walter Byron, Boris Karloff, and Mischa Auer); *The Cuban Love Song*, one of the few MGM films to play the theatre, a lovely, tuneful musical with Lawrence Tibbett, Lupe Velez, and Jimmy Durante, and *Delicious*, a Janet Gaynor-Charles Farrell musical with a George Gershwin score.

In 1932, along with the Charlie Chan mysteries, Will Rogers comedies, and brisk comedy-melodramas starring Spencer Tracy, Joan Bennett, James Dunn, or Warner Baxter, the Roxy occasionally booked a top-drawer film. For its fifth anniversary show, the theatre presented MGM's gangster melodrama, *Beast of the City*, with Walter Huston and Jean Harlow. Universal's version of the George S. Kaufman-Moss Hart stage comedy, *Once in a Lifetime*, with Aline MacMahon and Jack Oakie, was a broadly funny movie but it ran at the Roxy for only a week in October.

By 1933 the pinch of the Depression was being felt by every movie theatre, no matter how opulent. In February of that year, the Roxy inaugurated a new policy, lowering the price of admission and replacing its elaborate stage revues with vaudeville acts. Reporting on the first show under this policy, *The New York Times'* critic wrote, "The effect on the performers was electric. Rhythms quickened, feet kicked higher and faster, songs were sung with a new dash and jokes cracked with a new fervor." The feature film was not quite so electric: *The Death Kiss*, a murder mystery with Bela Lugosi, David Manners, and Adrienne Ames.

The movies shown throughout 1933 were mostly low-budget entries designed to fill the time between vaudeville acts. Typical titles were: *Pleasure Cruise*, with Genevieve Tobin and Roland Young, *Arizona to Broadway*, with James Dunn and Joan Bennett, *Flying Devils*, with Arline Judge and Bruce Cabot, *Her First Mate*, with Slim Summerville and ZaSu Pitts, and *Shanghai Madness*, with Spencer Tracy and Fay Wray. One special occasion (although the one week's run seems to indicate that the management hardly regarded it as special) was the showing, in March, of the classic *King Kong*. The movie opened simultaneously at the new Radio City Music Hall,

where it also ran for a week. *The New York Times'* critic called it "decidedly compelling," adding that "needless to say, this picture was received by many a giggle to cover up fright."

Its glorious trappings largely intact, the Roxy Theatre entered the heart of the Depression, carrying on through the balance of the thirties with mainly Fox films. (The prestigious Fox movies went to the Music Hall.)

* * * *

For Samuel Lionel Rothafel, the Roxy had been the culmination of a life-long dream. A onetime Marine, dishwasher, book peddler, ballplayer, and bartender, he had joined radio in its early years and from November 1922, had been a highly popular radio personality. ("Hello, everybody, this is Roxy speaking.") By 1923

The Roxy in its first year

he had assembled a permanent troupe of singers and musicians known as Roxy's Gang. Along with music and chatter, he would read letters from listeners and occasionally launch campaigns for good causes. One of his campaigns was to provide every patient in every veterans' hospital in the country with a small radio and earphones. All the time he kept dreaming of creating his own theatre.

When Herbert Lubin, a former film producer, bought the site of the Roxy, he needed a visionary to build on the property and he found one in Samuel Rothafel. Rothafel was made president of the company and had his final show with Roxy's Gang on July 25th, 1925. Later that year, in an interview in the *New York Morning Telegraph*, he said, "The Roxy will be the fulfillment of my dreams of the last fifteen years. I will be the absolute despot of it. I have always wanted to present pictures as I think they should be presented, and with the opening of the Roxy Theatre, I shall be hampered in no way whatsoever in having complete control over every detail, no matter how large or small."

The project ran into financial troubles until William Fox bought a controlling interest in the corporation for five million dollars. "The Cathedral of the Motion Picture" was finally opened to the public, although a plan for additional theatres to make up a Roxy circuit never came to pass.

In 1930 Roxy had another vision of an even greater, more elaborate theatre. The Radio City Music Hall was to be the most opulent movie palace of all. Again he and his staff worked feverishly and the theatre opened on December 27, 1932 with Frank Capra's *The Bitter Tea of General Yen* and an extravagant stage show that went on until 2:30 A.M. So many things went disastrously wrong that Roxy collapsed, critically ill. Pushed out of the corporation by "interim" management, he became a stunned, dismayed, ultimately broken man and died on January 13, 1936.

In the summer of 1960, the Roxy Theatre, Samuel Rothafel's "fairyland of novelty, comfort and convenience," his "magician's workshop . . . castle of the giants," was torn to the ground:

"The Roxy Theatre vanished in a pile of rubble and dust and some shards of gold-leafed plaster of Paris. Fallow ground where only an office building could grow marked the realm where fantasy flourished, where music and charm united us all to worship at beauty's throne."*

It was gone, but the memory of the golden age of the movie palace, the glitter of lights, the blare of music, the extravagant yet endearing foolishness of the entire enterprise, lingered amidst the rubble and dust.

* Ben M. Hall, *The Best Remaining Seats* (New York: Clarkson N. Potter, 1961), p. 258.

SATURDAY MARATHON
AT THE MOVIES

By William Wolf

Seeing films in screening rooms as a critic may be considered chic, but it doesn't begin to compare with the fun we used to have at the movies on Saturday afternoons when I was growing up in the small town of Bound Brook, New Jersey, during the 1930s. When one left home and headed for old faithful, the Brook Theatre, it was practically like going on a vacation trip. Our parents were just as happy.

The doors opened at about noon. We rushed to be among the first in the hope of finding seats down front. The eye doctors in town should have done a booming business. Since films weren't in CinemaScope then, if you sat in the first few rows, at least you didn't have to get bug-eyed looking side to side. You merely boggled at the enormous images before you and suffered a stiff

neck from looking up. Getting there early also provided an opportunity to say hello to all your friends, start a few fights, and yell for the show to begin. It was axiomatic that the program never started unless you shouted loudly and impatiently enough.

After the lights dimmed, the program generally began with cartoons. Popeye would devour his spinach, or Betty Boop might squeal through her assorted problems. Then lo and behold, the awaited serial. The episode might involve Flash Gordon zooming through outer space and the Emperor Ming plotting his evil deeds. We rarely got pictures when they first came out. They turned up any time. We might be looking at some decrepit Rin Tin Tin serials. Anything was welcome, as long as there was plenty of action or some laughs. Inevitably there would

also be a short, perhaps Andy Clyde bumbling through life. If we were unlucky, there would be one of those dull, educational pictures about some far-off place, or some new achievement, and we always made sure to boo. Naturally there was a newsreel. An announcer would intone the details of the latest disasters, a more jovial commentator would describe a beauty contest, and Lew Lehr would tell us about monkeys being "the *cwaziest* people." We didn't have television in those days, so the newsreels were an exciting window on the world.

Let's not forget the coming attractions for Tues. and Wed., Thurs. and Fri., and Sat., Sun., and Mon. These were a show in themselves—loud, enticing, and entertaining. They enabled you to begin lining up your arguments for using at home to permit going to the show on a school night. Dish night was a cinch for me. My grandmother wanted to go to keep up the set of dishes the theatre was doling out each week, and since my grandfather generally thought pictures were a waste of time, I could "escort" my grandmother and get an extra night at the movies that way.

Ultimately we'd get down to the double feature. If we heard the "rooty-toot" music signalling a Laurel and Hardy epic, there would be a deafening roar of approving whistles. The same would happen if it were a Western. A drama would be something we endured while waiting for a comedy, Western, or action film. Gangster pictures were sure winners. Musicals were favorites too, as were pictures that would scare the daylights out of us.

Memory plays tricks, and the mind doesn't readily sort out the sequences, or remember which films were billed together, or which played on Saturdays and which ones showed up during the week. Often the weaker double bills were on Saturdays because the management and distributors knew they had a captive audience anyhow. But those were days of movies that held great charisma for us, and the stars had a magical impact. We didn't only respond to the star performers in the leading roles. We recognized the faces we saw over and over again, and the minute they came on screen we knew the kind of part they were portraying—people like Guy Kibbee, Otto Kruger, Edgar Kennedy, Allen Jenkins, Henry Armetta, Gabby Hayes, Ruth Donnelly, Billie Burke.

We were eager mimics. If we saw Edward G. Robinson in *Little Caesar*, we'd leave the theatre vying to see

who could imitate him best. Or we'd make like James Cagney in *G-Men*. We'd try to talk like Warner Oland in the series of Charlie Chan films that were definite favorites, open our mouths as wide as possible after watching Joe E. Brown, give the jungle cry of Tarzan, or walk around trying to resemble King Kong or the monster in *Frankenstein*. We'd try to repeat the dialogue of Groucho and Chico Marx or the antics of Harpo after having seen *A Night at the Opera* or *A Day at the Races*.

Our Western heroes were William Boyd as "Hopalong Cassidy" and Ken Maynard in his movies. We were receptive to some of the films aimed at youngsters, such as *Treasure Island* or Shirley Temple in pictures like *Little Miss Marker* or *Heidi*. We enjoyed adventures, such as Errol Flynn in *The Charge of the Light Brigade*, or movies with lots of excitement, like *A Tale of Two Cities*. The *Broadway Melody* and *Big Broadcast* musicals had their appeal, but we thought Dick Powell could be sticky in a picture like *Flirtation Walk*. It was fun to be scared by *The Cat Creeps*, or by *Dr. Jekyll and Mr. Hyde*, but it was a point of honor to see a film like *Frankenstein* or *Dracula*. We didn't have any X, R, PG, or G ratings in those days. Occasionally a film would come to town and be forbidden to children, such as *Ecstasy*, with Hedy Lamarr momentarily nude. But nothing like that would ever play Saturday afternoons.

After the two features—yes, there was sometimes more—we might see vaudeville. Talent was cheap during the Depression. The theatre, when it indulged in vaudeville, would have a small orchestra and an array of performers making their way along the assorted vaudeville circuits that existed before television demolished them. We were a tough, fickle audience. We generously applauded tap dancers, particularly if they sweated a lot, but ballroom-style exhibitions were merely tolerated. Singers had a rougher time, especially if they dared venture into anything resembling a classic. But a high note reached without faltering usually drew applause out of respect.

Magicians were generally greeted with calls of "It's a fake" or "I know how you did that one." Comics were on stage at their own risk. It was more fun not to laugh at them. Better still, if we stayed for the second show in the evening, we could shout the punch lines before a comic could deliver them. "Don't you have a home?" a comedian called out in desperation to one brat. Eventually, as economic conditions improved, vaudeville was cut to fewer acts, and we thought that was a cheat. And then there were none at all.

After the stage show came the raffle. Something was given away each Saturday to the lucky holder of the winning ticket stub. For one period they were giving away motor bikes, balloon-tired bicycles with motors

attached. We never seemed to know the person who won. On the way out of the theatre we would be handed our free ice cream. Sometimes the bonus would be a packet of stamps—a different package each week to enhance the collections we had been started on.

The ticket price for all of the foregoing was fifteen cents for children—if we didn't sneak in. Some kids would brazenly try to break in through the side exit doors, but that would bring an usher or the manager hurrying down the aisle to seize the culprits and toss them back into the alley. The more sophisticated method was to purchase a ticket, and since the management used the same color tickets for long periods of time, try to hold on to it. You waited until a group of people, preferably tall, went in, and then you attempted to slither by without the ticket taker noticing. If he did, you could nonchalantly give him the ticket. If not, the ticket could be held for a similar gambit the following week. My record for keeping the same ticket was twelve Saturdays in a row.

Happily, there were no matrons to annoy us once we were inside. Nobody appeared to care if we raced up and down the aisles to the bathroom, or if we gave a raspberry to adults telling us to shut up. Ushers would only break up the fights that got out of hand. You never threw gum in a trash can. Its proper place when you finished a few hours of chewing was under your seat,

on the back of the seat in front of you, and occasionally in the hair of a friend.

Looking back now, I realize that we white kids never pondered an unwritten rule that black kids were expected to sit in the back of the theatre or on the side. We didn't question it, and I can't recall any community protest of the situation, although there surely must have been some. And this was in the North. There was no such thing as the black action film then. On screen Stepin Fetchit shuffled, Willie Best gaped in fright, and Bill Robinson grinned and rolled his eyes as he danced.

After the movie orgy, we'd make our way home with friends and rehash what we had seen. "Remember when the guy said . . . . How about the part where he shoots the other guy . . . . The comedian was lousy . . . . The magician should learn some new tricks." We'd gallop through the streets slapping our rumps to make the sound of a horse. We'd pretend to fight with swords as if we were little Errol Flynns.

If we were lucky, we'd get to a show again during the week. For some of us, the only game in town was to try to see everything that came to the Brook. Eventually, another theatre called the Lyric also opened, and that one played films the Brook didn't get, so we had two show "palaces" to visit. Of course, going to the movies midweek was never as enjoyable for me as on Saturday afternoons, and it will never be like that again.

Jackie Cooper places his handprints in cement at Grauman's Chinese Theatre, December 12, 1931. (Courtesy Academy of Motion Picture Arts and Sciences)

THE GOLDEN MOVIE PALACES
OF HOLLYWOOD

By Foster Hirsch

In the days when movies were young and later when they first learned to talk, going to the movies was an occasion. The way films were presented, and the magnificent theatres that were constructed in their honor, gave dignity to the new popular art. Built in the teens, the twenties, and the thirties, the "temples of the motion picture art" were often more entertaining than the films that filled their screens and the vaudeville shows that sprawled over their enormous stages.

The motion picture cathedrals afford a unique glimpse into another era's taste. To the modern temper, the movie palaces are preposterously ornate; with their huge vaulted lobbies, their cavernous, intricately detailed auditoriums, their proudly embellished prosceniums and ceilings, their showpiece chandeliers, the grand old theatres are an offense to the contemporary taste for streamlined glass boxes. Like the movies themselves, the palaces have lost most of their audience. Many of the theatres have been torn down to make room for parking lots or skyscrapers; the remaining houses are outrageously oversized for a shrinking moviegoing public.

The old theatres were built in downtown areas that are also no longer what they used to be, and these vast theatres in decaying neighborhoods cannot compete for new films with the suburban shopping center shoeboxes. While the remaining Main Street Orpheums and Rialtos are reduced to showing black exploitation programmers and Kung Fu triple bills, the latest "in" films play in soulless mini-cinemas in areas that are as safe and antiseptic as the theatres themselves.

I was lucky enough to grow up near Hollywood during the fifties and early sixties, and I can boast of many Saturday afternoons at the four movie palaces of Hollywood Boulevard: the Egyptian, the Chinese, the Warners, and the Pantages. Unlike many theatres of comparable splendor, the Hollywood houses still stand, un-subdivided. At each of the theatres there has been some foolish tampering, some remodeling and draping, but many of their architectural details are still on view. The theatres have faced some rough booking periods during which they have had to play revivals or double bills, but the four showplaces can still claim a proud, if somewhat dimmed, first-run status.

These theatres are all that remain of the Old Hollywood. Tourists who come to see the fabled "Hollywood" are always disappointed—"Hollywood" lives in Beverly Hills, and the Boulevard that was once, briefly, a gathering place and shopping mecca for the stars looks now like almost any other seedy Main Street with its plastic burger joints, its cut-rate bargain stores, and its contingent of wretched and bedraggled night people. Only the "Sidewalk of the Stars," some movie memorabilia shops, and the majestic theatres are reminders that the thoroughfare belongs to the one-time motion picture capital of the world.

With their showy architecture that befits the public's idealized view of what "Hollywood" should be, the theatres can claim a genuine part in Hollywood history. The houses were built by showmen who themselves became celebrities and who planned their theatres as monuments to their fame.

Sid Grauman was the most famous and beloved of the theatre owners. Known in the trade as "Little Sunshine," he knew the town; producers and stars adored him. Grauman, in fact, was as much a personality and star in his own right as it's possible for a theatre owner to become. Grauman's motto was "to lighten the burden of the toilworn members of the human race who seek relaxation in opera chairs." To that end, Grauman built a chain of sumptuous, distinctive theatres in which to stage vaudeville shows and to present movies. Each Grauman theatre had its own "enlarged" symphony orchestra and its own Wurlitzer organ. The Grauman stage shows were renowned not only for their spectacle but also for the fact that they were always designed as prologues to the movie: they were "theme" shows whose pageants were lavish, stylized comments, sometimes satirical, more often respectful, on the feature film. In his prime in the twenties, Grauman published his own *Grauman's Theatres Magazine* which proudly listed the complete vaudeville offerings at each of the theatres and which contained *Photoplay*-style interviews and snippets of Hollywood gossip.

Grauman built his first theatre in 1918 on Broadway in downtown Los Angeles.* With a bow to the city's heritage, the Million Dollar Theatre displayed a flamboyant Spanish Baroque architecture. Grauman soon added

---

* In the teens and twenties, Broadway was Los Angeles' Great White Way. Almost all of the grand vaudfilm houses remain, one more elaborate than the other. The Orpheum, the Palace, the Million Dollar, the Tower, the State, the United Artists, and (best of all) the renowned Los Angeles provide a movie palace fan's delight.

Grauman's Million Dollar Theatre in 1919 (Courtesy Academy of Motion Picture Arts and Sciences)

the Rialto and, in early 1923, the Metropolitan, which was billed as "the most magnificent theatre edifice in history."* Theatre historians claim that there has never been anything quite like the Metropolitan; whereas the Fox and Orpheum palaces were plush, the Metropolitan's grandeur was decidedly austere. The basic color was cement gray rather than the customary gold or red, and the walls were bare, rough concrete. The theatre was built as "a monument to the casualties of the World War" and Grauman boasted that the design was intended to represent "the grinding of cosmic forces let loose by the war."

Eccentric as it was, the Metropolitan never became as famous as Grauman's two Hollywood showcases, the Egyptian and the Chinese. As early as 1923, Grauman realized that Hollywood would surpass downtown Los Angeles as a moviegoing area, and he engaged the architectural team of Meyer and Holler to create a theatre that would be worthy of its Hollywood setting. The Egyptian motif was suggested by the Metropolitan, whose modernity had a faintly pagan underpinning.

* After Grauman sold it in the mid-twenties, the Metropolitan became the Paramount. (*Bwana Devil*, the first 3-D film, world premiered at the theatre in 1953.) The Paramount was torn down in 1960 to make way for a parking lot.

The Egyptian ("where the stars see the pictures") opened its carved doors in grand style on October 18, 1923, with Douglas Fairbanks in *Robin Hood*. For the occasion, Grauman invented the Hollywood premiere. Grauman operated the theatre on a reserved-seat, two-a-day basis; the box office was open from 10 A.M. to 10 P.M. and seats were on sale one week in advance. Grauman was proud of his long runs; after *Robin Hood,* he booked *The Covered Wagon* and then *The Ten Commandments,* each of which played the prestige house for many months.

An irrepressible showman, Grauman competed with DeMille in presenting *The Ten Commandments* to the public. Publicity linked the theatre to the picture: *"The Ten Commandments* is DeMille's supreme effort . . . the Grauman's Hollywood Egyptian is a fitting frame. Both are triumphs of art." For the DeMille epic, Grauman assembled a stage show that rivalled the Master in its pomp and splendor and its mixture of sex and religious uplift. From the Dancing Favorites of Pharaoh to a tableau of The Last Supper, the show was a heady blend of pagan and Christian spectacle.

The theatre's doors were shaped like entrances to a pyramid. On the parapet above the entrance, a Bedouin in robes chanted the name of the film. Along the arcade leading from Hollywood Boulevard to the theatre were hand-painted murals of stylized Egyptian figures. Inside, the proscenium was framed by massive pillars, and over the proscenium was a spectacular sunburst effect. The rest of the auditorium, however, departed from the architectural customs of the time in being surpassingly plain. The walls had a desert-like stone texture, only occasionally highlighted by colorful Egyptian designs.

Today the proscenium arch is gone, replaced by anonymous drapery, but the ceiling and the walls are intact. The lobby has been completely changed, and the arcade retains only faint suggestions of its former glory. Standing guard near the two principal doors leading to the auditorium are jackals that were used in *Cleopatra*; the mummy that graces the lobby is on permanent loan from Twentieth Century-Fox. Still regal at fifty-two, the Egyptian has had booking problems since 1970 and now seems fated to increasingly undistinguished fare—a far cry from Grauman's original concept for the theatre.

Grauman's greatest moment was the opening on May 18, 1927, of his most illustrious theatre, "the world-famous Chinese." Theatre historians assert that "if the Roxy is the cathedral of the motion picture, Grauman's Chinese is its High Pagoda." The Chinese is a delightful theatre, brighter and more playful than the sober Egyptian. Of course, it's as "Chinese" as the Egyptian is "Egyptian"—both theatres are strictly Hollywood versions of ancient civilizations. While the Egyptian motifs stress royal processions, the Chinese decor features dragons, flames and brooding masks. Two great stone dogs guard the entrance. The walls of the foyer present a more delicate view of ancient Chinese life; flowers and gardens and pastoral scenes delight the eye. The main auditorium is framed on both sides by thick columns that reach to the ceiling, but the effect is light and airy rather than massive. The opening-night program contended that the huge, wide auditorium "gives the impression of entering a gigantic shrine of the time of the Five Emperors or the dynasty of Hsia, when the world was very young."

The Chinese looks expensive. It towers over Hollywood Boulevard, and both inside and out, its lines soar upward. And yet for all the heavy stone walls and thick columns and rugs, the effect is delicate and charming. The theatre's design is good-natured kitsch, corniness eager to please.

In addition to its fairy-tale architecture, which embellishes "the mystery of the Orient" with a distinctly Southern California exaggeration, the theatre is famed for its elliptical forecourt with its galaxy of footprints of the Hollywood great. The footprint idea happened quite by accident: one afternoon in the spring of 1927, Grauman

took Norma Talmadge to see the progress being made on his theatre. Miss Talmadge stepped by mistake into a block of newly poured cement, leaving her footprints. Grauman seized on the imprint as the appropriate accompaniment to the theatre that he was building as a tribute to Hollywood.

Grauman's program for the theatre's opening attraction of DeMille's *King of Kings* was his most flamboyant. His "Glories of the Scriptures" prologue, with its procession of prayers and dances and chants and tableaux, matched DeMille spectacle for spectacle. Grauman's opening night line-up was worthy of "the dedicatory premiere of a playhouse whose fame is already spread to the four corners of the world." Director Fred Niblo introduced D. W. Griffith who introduced Will H. Hays who introduced America's Beloved Star Miss Mary Pickford who "formally started" the evening's performance.

Grauman presented his last stage show in 1938 (the special feature of which was the appearance on either side of the stage of two naked girls). The theatre had a spotty history during the forties, but since the early fifties, the Chinese has been an exclusive first-run showcase. The theatre was the home of Fox CinemaScope epics in the fifties, and the opening-night ceremonies for *The Robe* in 1953 were the brightest the place had seen since 1927.

The third deluxe Hollywood movie house added a Spanish touch to the Boulevard. Built in 1928 as "a monument to the ambitions and struggles of a family of pioneers," the Warner Hollywood (now the Pacific) was designed as a "Castle in Spain." "This is no theatre auditorium," the opening-night program trumpeted, "we are in the garden of some noble castle high in the hills of Spain." Unfortunately, in a senseless fifties remodeling, the auditorium's arcade of pillars, its panorama of painted trees and turreted roofs and soaring hills, and its azure vaulted ceiling were draped and covered over. But the spectacular lobby remains untouched. Designed as a wide semicircular promenade, the lobby is distinguished by its array of graceful pillars and columns and arches, its gold inlaid hand-painted ceiling, its intricately decorated chandeliers, and its massive wood-paneled doors leading to the auditorium. The promenade is a riot of neo-Renaissance detail.

The Warner Hollywood was built to celebrate the Warners' introduction of the Vitaphone ("the spoken film play"). The theatre was dedicated as the flagship house for "the crowning achievement of all screen history—the Warner Brothers' Vitaphone." Al Jolson was master of ceremonies on opening night, but the Warners' claim that their grand Spanish Renaissance house was to play only the best of the spoken films was belied by the premiere engagement of Dolores Costello in *Glorious Betsy*.

An aerial view of Hollywood Boulevard in 1948, with Grauman's Chinese Theatre in the foreground (Courtesy Academy of Motion Picture Arts and Sciences)

Like the other Hollywood cathedrals, the Warner prospered in the fifties, when Hollywood went fancy in order to compete with television. It was Fox Cinema-Scope at the Chinese, MGM reserved-seat epics at the Egyptian, and Cinerama at the Warner. The lavish, massive theatre was the perfect setting for the Cinerama travelogues. Since Cinerama days, the theatre has had a sporadic history; between blockbusters like *Airport* and *A Clockwork Orange,* the theatre has had to get by with double bills, subruns, and even a few soft-core packages.

The last Hollywood palace was built in 1930 as a personal monument to Alexander Pantages. Like Grauman, Pantages made money in the Alaska gold rush, and he too moved down the coast from San Francisco to Los Angeles. Pantages, who was Greek-born and who never learned to read or write, was a vaudeville entrepreneur who fearlessly moved into the Orpheum territory. In his heyday, Pantages ran the most important independent vaudeville circuit in the country. The Pantages "time" was famous for its lengthy bookings, often as long as thirty-two weeks. But unlike Grauman, Pantages wasn't very good at making friends. Because he fought the powerful Orpheum circuit, he sometimes faced a shortage of acts. Because he didn't have Grauman's rapport with movie producers, he didn't always get the best films to show in his theatres.

Pantages prospered throughout the twenties, but the '29 crash dismantled his empire. He sold his splendid Downtown Los Angeles Theatre (now a church) to the Warners and his six other principal theatres to his former rivals, Radio-Keith-Orpheum. After the sale, Pantages wanted to construct a last monument to his name, and like Sid Grauman and the Warners, he chose Hollywood as the appropriate location. To design his theatre, Pantages engaged B. Marcus Priteca, who had been his architect since 1911.

All of Pantages' former theatres had been fanciful adaptations of the Greek style. (The enormous theatres were jokingly referred to as Pantages Greek.) But for the Hollywood Pantages, the showman wanted something different. Priteca, who was the most respected of all movie palace architects, designed a theatre that historians have called "the most strikingly elaborate modern theatre ever built." The Hollywood Pantages isn't Greek; it isn't Oriental or Spanish or Italian. It doesn't look like a Fox or a Paramount or an Orpheum. It's a mixture of all of these. Blending elements of baroque and modern, it is an extravagant, bizarre, sweeping statement, a series of soaring architectural gestures that resemble a set from *Intolerance* or a DeMille epic. The vast vaulted grand lobby is 110 feet wide by 60 feet deep. The auditorium has a double ceiling; a series of sun-ray effects converge in the center, from which hangs a mammoth chandelier. Above all is a sky blue ceiling. The intricate details of the proscenium arch are carried throughout the interior. A series of for-show-only balconies surrounds the auditorium on either side. Priteca didn't leave an empty corner; his design is a chaos of triangles and pyramids, arches and squares and circles. Murals, paintings, sculptures, and bas-relief figures throughout the theatre portray a variety of subjects, ranging from Greek mythology to Roman history to American pioneers.

Unlike the other Hollywod theatres, which are remarkable for their lightweight atmosphere, the Pantages is somber, brooding. The Chinese winks at you; the Pantages takes its grandeur seriously. The present Pacific management appreciates Priteca's genius, and they have recently re-gold-leafed the exquisite details. As a result, the Pantages looks almost the same as it did on opening night in 1930 when it presented Marion Davies in *The Floradora Girl.*

If I had my way, these Hollywood palaces and similar theatres all over the country would be reinstated as deluxe first-run showcases. And if I had my way further, the major studios, from time to time, would again make spectacular movies that the palaces are ideally equipped to present, four-hour Roman epics, biblical extravaganzas, and historical romances that deserve to be shown in luxurious settings. But that kind of movie, like the wonderful old theatres themselves, are a part of Hollywood history that can be fondly remembered but never repeated.

THE "NABES"

By Ted Sennett

The raucous cheers and applause of children as an arrogant Nazi flyer is shot down in flames. The crackle of candy wrappers. The indignant cry of a hulking "matron" as she tries to keep a boy from twisting the braids of the girl in front of him. The ear-assaulting blare of the "previews of coming attractions."

These are the sounds of my moviegoing past, and the past of every devoted film buff who grew up in the dark, slightly dank but nonetheless magical atmosphere of the "neighborhood" moviehouse in the heart of Brooklyn, New York. Yes, there were the film "palaces"—the vast, cathedral-like arenas where the glitter of the walls and ceilings was matched only by the glitter of the ushers' uniforms. But attending these mammoth theatres was not really "going to the movies"; they were occasional pilgrimages to a shrine where the music from the giant organ, the ritualistic raising of the huge velvet curtain, and the dazzling image of the goddess-in-residence (Betty Grable or Olivia de Havilland) all conspired to create an exhilarating experience.

Our movie-loving hearts and minds belonged to the neighborhood theatres or "nabes," as *Variety* called them, to the Claridge and the Highway and the Avalon and the Jewel, where once a week (and sometimes twice) all the neighborhood children would converge for a viewing of two feature films, a batch of color cartoons, a chapter from a serial, several previews of coming attractions, a few local announcements, and occasionally a "live" extra: the raffling of a turkey, or a bicycle, or free movie tickets. With a decibel level that might give a dog a nervous breakdown, with the odors of melted butter, Juicy Fruit gum and perhaps an overripe banana wafting through the theatre, an afternoon at the local Bijou was not exactly a cultural occasion. But somehow, out of the catcalls, the whistles, and the pelted popcorn came a pleasure that doesn't fade in memory and, curiously, a deep and abiding love of "the movies."

In the thirties and forties, when most of my neighborhood moviegoing took place, the price of admission ranged from a dime to a quarter. As I grew taller, and the likelihood of my passing for a child under twelve diminished with every passing month, I would stoop down at the cashier's window and timidly place my coin before her, my fingers barely reaching the window. Usually she would cast a baleful eye on this pathetic midget and let me pass, to the obvious amusement of the doorman, who saw a sprouting pre-teenager. Occasionally she would ask me to pay the adult's price, which left me without candy money.

Inside the theatre, I would join a host of other children engaged in their usual activities: shrieking, pummeling each other, purchasing boxes of Goober's, Jujubes, Good 'n Plenty, or nonpareils, racing down the aisles at bullet speed, or working industriously at routing or discomfiting the Enemy. The Enemy was the "matron," a hard-faced woman built along the lines of Hope Emerson, whose unenviable job was to keep a semblance of order among this rowdy group by using threats, mild arm-twisting, and a voice that could penetrate steel. Since she was regarded with about as much warmth as a concentration camp inmate viewed Ilse Koch, it was the sworn duty of the children to keep her on the move, busy with separating the battlers, warning the rowdiest offenders, and keeping the debris to any weight under a ton. She usually came armed with a whistle and occasionally with another matron.

Once the noise had changed from an ear-splitting roar to a conversational hum, the theatre was darkened and the film program began. After a few commercial messages from local merchants and a stern warning to the tots that smoking was not allowed, the cartoons were run in a cluster: Looney Tunes with Daffy Duck, Bugs Bunny, and Elmer Fudd; Disney cartoons with Donald Duck and Goofy; the antics of Popeye and his gang. We enjoyed them all, laughing appreciatively at their blissful absurdity and paying no heed to their bloodless violence and

Alice Faye and Betty Grable in TIN PAN ALLEY (1940)

FLASH GORDON (1936). Buster Crabbe is taken prisoner.

destruction. (There may have been a budding psychologist in the audience, fretting about the possibly harmful effects of the cartoons, but he was probably laughing as hard as the others.) I was particularly fond of Daffy Duck, that unflappable lunatic who continually escaped disaster by a mere feather.

The cartoons were usually followed by a chapter of a serial, another ludicrous but spine-tingling episode in a continuing cliff-hanger. Here, Dick Tracy would be trapped in the lair of a masked villain who would attempt to deep-fry him in a vat of boiling oil. Or he would be hurled from a steep cliff by a burly adversary. Or Captain Marvel would work to thwart the evil designs of the Scorpion and his Golden Scorpion Atom Smasher. Or a group of intrepid travelers would find themselves prisoners on a volcanic island dominated by a devilish villain bent on controlling the immediate ·world. Though we knew that the satanic forces were no match for Buster Crabbe or Ralph Byrd, we cringed and shrieked as each episode found the hero in mortal peril. None of us paid the slightest attention to the dialogue; we were all willing slaves of the special-effects men. And if the effects were obviously fake, we pretended not to notice.

A brief but favorite feature was the preview of coming attractions, an art that may be well lost but which contributed to the afternoon's pleasure. While we dipped into our second box of Good 'n Plenty, we were regaled with news about upcoming films: a "monumental epic three years in the making" in which "romance triumphs amid the ruins of a monster hurricane." We were given tantalizing Technicolor glimpses of Carmen Miranda cavorting in the tropics or Esther Williams emerging like a water-logged Venus from a lagoon filled with chorus girls. We were exhorted to "See!," to "Watch!," to "Listen!" We were greeted by the queenly presence of Joan Crawford or Greer Garson telling us "sincerely" about the special moving quality of her latest film, or by the sinister presence of the portly Sydney Greenstreet, inviting us to share "a tale of unspeakable terror." Happily we knew we would be back next week to "see," to "watch," to "listen."

At long last we arrived at the feature films. By this time most of us had consumed our candy, had reached an uneasy peace with the matron, and had made several trips to the bathroom. Now we were ready to watch Errol Flynn or Tyrone Power leap from parapets and fight their duels, to see Jimmy Cagney gun down his victims, to admire Alice Faye and Betty Grable in spangled tights, singing their hearts out for John Payne or Don Ameche, while Jack Oakie looked on, his moon-face beaming. We were waiting to laugh at Abbott and Costello, or Mickey Rooney, or the Marx Brothers.

There were, however, things we refused to accept, things to which we reacted with derision or noisy inattention. One was Love. The hero's light peck on the heroine's dewy cheek would cause nervous giggles. Even a tentative embrace would produce laughter. And a passionate love scene would be met with scornful howls and a barrage of popcorn pellets. One boy would shout, "Cut the mush!" and another, bolder boy would cry, "Go get 'er, Zorro!" At this point, the matron would be approaching apoplexy.

We also had very little regard for lengthy exposition. Madeleine Carroll and Ian Hunter discussing their family's checkered history of the last ten years, Thomas Mitchell explaining about his amnesia, or Barbara Stanwyck telling Joan Fontaine why she must give up Walter Pidgeon —these conversational scenes were usually inaudible as we waited for the next plane crash, the next spurting of blood, the next lavish musical number, the next scream of joy or wail of anguish. The subtler pleasures of movie-going were not for us, and we made our preferences known, vociferously.

We endured a certain amount of sentiment—a lost dog, a disrupted home—though we liked to think of it as "sticky" or "gooey." However, we would simply not tolerate the sentiment that degenerated into bathos. If a scene was clearly designed to drain the audience of every tear, to play on easily aroused emotions, we gave it our laughter. I think we may have been wiser than adults to the overwrought deathbed scene, the hysterical forced separations of parent and child, and all the other hoary devices of moviemakers.

When the program was over and we filed (or actually hurtled) out of the theatre, we were happily praising or castigating the films we had seen. ("Wasn't it great when he knifed the spy?" "Watta lousy movie!") We had sat (or squirmed or rushed about) for three-and-a-half or four hours in a darkened theatre, pleased to have shared a communal experience with our friends. We were satiated with "eye-popping thrills," "toe-tapping musical joy," dreams of glory—and candy.

The serials have gone. The previews of coming attractions have become more "dignified," more "sincere." The cartoons linger on, but most of the feature films are *not* for children, and many of them are not for adults, either.

The neighborhood theatres of my past were often shabby, ill-run, and haphazard in their approach to programming. But my lasting love affair with the movies that continues today in the sanitary, well-managed theatres of suburbia began in those "nabes" so many years ago.

STILL MORE MOVIE MATTERS

Little-known facts about some well-known players, plus some random reflections on the vagaries of the movies.

In his first sound film, *The Jazz Age* (1929), Joel McCrea was billed in sixth place, below stars Douglas Fairbanks, Jr. and Marceline Day. Robert Montgomery made his sound debut in *So This Is College* (1929), as a college youth vying with Elliott Nugent for co-ed Sally Starr. Walter Pidgeon made his film debut as the sympathetic hero of Fannie Hurst's *Mannequin* (1926), starring Dolores Costello.

Fay Wray, the immortal screamer of *King Kong,* had already appeared in *nineteen* sound films before *Kong.* Her first sound movie was the third version of A. E. W. Mason's novel, *Four Feathers,* with Richard Arlen, William Powell, and Clive Brook.

You're Never Too Old: Edmund Gwenn made his sound feature debut at the age of fifty-six in *How He Lied to Her Husband,* (1931). Monty Woolley was forty-nine when he appeared in his first movie, *Live, Love and Learn* (1937). Sydney Greenstreet was sixty-two when he made his auspicious debut in *The Maltese Falcon* (1941). George Arliss was sixty-one when he starred in his first sound feature film, *Disraeli* (1929). S. Z. Sakall was fifty-five when he made his first American film, *It's a Date* (1940). Florence Bates was fifty-two when she made her memorable film debut as the snobbish Mrs. Van Hopper in *Rebecca* (1940).

George Arliss in DISRAELI (1929), with Joan Bennett

THEY KNEW WHAT THEY WANTED (1940). With William Gargan, Charles Laughton, and Carole Lombard

In 1929, a sound film called *The Song of Love* starred singer Belle Baker as a much put-upon woman with husband trouble. The blonde vamp who entrances the husband was played by a teen-aged actress named Eunice Quedens. Four years later, as a chorus girl in MGM's *Dancing Lady,* she was still billed as Eunice Quedens. In 1937 she changed her name to Eve Arden for *Oh, Doctor!* Incidentally, *Dancing Lady* marked the feature film debut of a number of players, including Fred Astaire, Nelson Eddy, and Lynn Bari.

Many films of the twenties and thirties were fond of titles that made flatly declarative statements about the whims, attitudes, and needs of women. These included: *Ladies Must Live* (1921), *Ladies Must Dress* (1927), *Ladies Beware* (1927), *Ladies Love Brutes* (1930), *Ladies Must Play* (1930), and *Ladies Should Listen* (1934). Also: *She Couldn't Help It* (1920), *She Couldn't Say No* (1930), *She Got What She Wanted* (1930), *She Wanted a Millionaire* (1932), *She Had to Say Yes* (1933), *She Had to Choose* (1934), *She Learned About Sailors* (1934), *She Made Her Bed* (1934), *She Was a Lady* (1934), and, as a fitting climax, *She Gets Her Man* (1935).

The 1972 stage revival of *No, No, Nanette* starred the raucous, hard-bitten Patsy Kelly as the maid Pauline. In *two* earlier film versions of the musical (1930 and 1940), the role was played by ZaSu Pitts, an actress whose vague and fluttery style could not be more different than Ms. Kelly's.

Sidney Howard's play, *They Knew What They Wanted,* has had a long stage and film history. The play opened in November, 1924 with Richard Bennett as Tony, the prosperous bootlegger who takes Amy, played by Pauline Lord, as his mail-order bride. It was first filmed by Paramount in 1928 as *The Secret Hour,* with Tony, now called Luigi (Jean Hersholt), changed into a respectable orange-grower who takes Pola Negri as his bride. In 1930 it was produced and directed by Victor Seastrom as *A Lady to Love,* with Edward G. Robinson, in his third sound film, as Tony and Vilma Banky as Amy. Here Tony became a tiller of the vine who consumes large quantities of his product. The next film version reverted to the play's original title and was released in 1940 by RKO. Under Garson Kanin's direction, Charles Laughton played Tony, again a grape grower, and Carole Lombard appeared as the mail-order bride. In 1956, Frank Loesser turned the story into a stage musical, *The Most Happy Fella,* with opera star Robert Weede as Tony and Jo Sullivan as Amy.

★ ★ ★ ★

THE DIVORCEE (1929). With Norma Shearer and Chester Morris

When did Lionel Barrymore, Lawrence Tibbett, Stan Laurel and Oliver Hardy work together in a movie? In 1930, when Barrymore directed Tibbett in *The Rogue Song*, adapted from Franz Lehar's operetta, *Gypsy Love*. Laurel and Hardy were the featured comedians in this Technicolor movie.

Another 1930 curiosity was Paramount's *Roadhouse Nights*, a comedy-drama concerning politics and bootlegging. The screenplay by Ben Hecht involved Charlie Ruggles as a reporter who exposes a Chicago liquor ring. He is saved from a gangster's bullet by singer Helen Morgan (in her first film after the famous *Applause*).

Featured in the cast were Jimmy Durante and his longtime partners Eddie Jackson and Lou Clayton.

In the third year of Academy Award contention (1929–1930), Norma Shearer won the Best Actress Award for *The Divorcée*, an MGM drama about a woman's marital and postmarital problems. She was also competing against herself for her performance in *Their Own Desire*, about a girl involved in her parents' divorce. Her co-star in both films was Robert Montgomery.

THE SWAN (1956). With Grace Kelly and Alec Guinness

THE LODGER (1944). Laird Cregar stalks victim Queenie Leonard.

Douglas Fairbanks, Jr. and Walter Pidgeon played the same role—eighteen years apart. In 1930, First National filmed *Bride of the Regiment,* a comedy with music based on an operetta, *The Lady in Ermine.* Vivienne Segal starred as a countess, with Walter Pidgeon as the dashing hussar who courts her. In 1948 it was remade by Fox as *That Lady in Ermine,* the last film directed by Ernst Lubitsch. Betty Grable played the countess and Douglas Fairbanks, Jr. played the hussar. (There was another version in 1927, with Corinne Griffith and Elnar Hanson.

★ ★ ★ ★

Ferenc Molnar's play, *The Swan,* had an interesting life in America. It was produced on Broadway in 1923, with Eva Le Gallienne, Basil Rathbone, and Philip Merivale in the leading roles. It was filmed under its original title in 1925, with Frances Howard (later Mrs. Samuel Goldwyn) as the heroine and Adolphe Menjou and Ricardo Cortez as her co-stars. In 1930, it was filmed as *One Romantic Night,* with Lillian Gish in her sound debut and Conrad Nagel and Rod La Rocque in support. The most recent version was MGM's *The Swan* in 1956, with Grace Kelly in her next-to-last role to date. Alec Guinness and Louis Jourdan were the male leads.

128

Anne Shirley was child actress Dawn O'Day until 1934 when she appeared in *Anne of Green Gables* and then took over the name of the character she played. Gig Young used his real name, Byron Barr, until he played a character named Gig Young in *The Gay Sisters* (1942) and took over that name. Actress May Wynn played a character called May Wynn in *The Caine Mutiny* (1954). She made only two other films, *The Violent Men* (1954) and *They Rode West* (1955).

In the fall of 1931, a British film turned up briefly and departed quickly. It was *The Speckled Band,* adapted from Sir Arthur Conan Doyle's Sherlock Holmes story. The detective was played by a newcomer to films, Canadian-born Raymond Massey. At the time the movie opened in New York City, Massey was appearing on stage as Hamlet. *The New York Times'* reviewer found his interpretation superior to Clive Brook's in *The Adventures of Sherlock Holmes,* two years earlier, but he never played the role again.

Alfred Hitchcock's British-made 1926 melodrama, *The Lodger,* concerning a man (Ivor Novello) who may or may not be Jack the Ripper, was not released in the United States until 1928, though it had been widely praised in England. For American showings, the title was changed to *The Case of Jonathan Drew,* and it was largely panned by *The New York Times'* critic as "unimpressive," with "a very, very excellent beginning, a mediocre middle, and a most deplorable ending." (The leading character is not Jack the Ripper at all, but a man seeking to trap the killer as revenge for murdering his sister.) Seven years later, the story was remade as *The Phantom Fiend,* with Ivor Novello repeating his role as the mysterious lodger, this time under the direction of Maurice Elvey. An American version, reverting to the original title of *The Lodger,* was released in 1944, with the splendidly hammy Laird Cregar in the leading role. Nine years later, the story was remade as *The Man in the Attic,* with Jack Palance in the title role under Hugo Fregonese's direction.

Nat Pendleton, the burly actor who started in films in 1924 and spent years playing amiable oafs—he was Sandow the Strong Man in *The Great Ziegfeld* and Wayman, the hospital orderly in MGM's "Dr. Kildare" series —was the Olympic heavyweight wrestling champion in 1923. In 1933 he wrote and starred in a Columbia film called *Deception,* in which he played a wrestler managed by Leo Carrillo who becomes involved with the manager's blonde mistress, Thelma Todd. (*The New York Times* remarked that, as the siren, "Thelma Todd appears to be under the impression that she is still leading lady for the Four Marx Brothers.")

129

FOUR:
THE PEOPLE BE-HIND THE CAMERA

Every film, from a shoestring "quickie" to a gargantuan epic, requires the combined effort of scores of skilled and conscientious people —and sometimes a few who are remarkably talented in their respective fields.

This section is dedicated to the people behind the camera who, except for a few master directors, seldom achieve public acclaim or even public notice. However, they play an indispensable role in creating the art of movie magic.

And speaking of movie magic, we begin with René Jordan's fascinating article on how some directors are adept at using legerdemain to weave award-winning performances out of thin air. . . .

"NOW YOU SEE IT, NOW YOU DON'T":

The Art of Movie Magic

By René Jordan

In the twenties, during the golden era of Soviet silent film, director Lev Kuleshov set up a bold experiment to prove his theories on the subliminal powers of *montage*. He selected a shot from an old movie made by matinee idol Ivan Mousjoukine and then spliced it with three odd strips of film, picked at random from the archives. For his editing feat, he used nothing but a close-up of Mousjoukine's blank face, intercut with frames showing a plate of food, a woman's breasts and a coffin.

Raw materials indeed, but enough to create film magic. The unvarying close-up instantly mutated into a trio of astounding reaction shots. When Kuleshov screened his sequences separately, each set of viewers commented on Mousjoukine's unlimited range of expression. How he hungered for the stew! How he lusted for the naked girl! How he grieved over the death of a loved one! Kuleshov then revealed the trick to prove his point, and at the same time offered a classic example of a film director's almost boundless control over his performers.

Kuleshov was a pioneer who pointed the way to treacherous territory. Over the years, as film techniques achieved hair-breadth perfection, directors learned to do nearly everything with their magic props of light, camera, and sound. They were even able to bring the dead back to life. Robert Walker passed away before the final scene of *My Son John* was shot, leaving director Leo McCarey with an unfinished picture. In despair, McCarey called Alfred Hitchcock and asked him for the negative of Walker's death scene under a carousel-gone-berserk in *Strangers on a Train*. When *My Son John* was finally released, as Walker writhes in agony, audiences had no idea they were watching a close-up from the previous Hitchcock movie, with director McCarey's own voice on the soundtrack, reciting the character's last impassioned speech.

Kuleshov's and McCarey's feats are extreme examples of "Now you see it, now you don't": the art of movie magic.

Tempered by everyday routine or exacerbated by eleventh-hour desperation, this kind of magic keeps flourishing in sets all over the world. It is a staple of movie witchcraft through the ages. Directors haunted by tight shooting schedules and unresponding actors often resort to an in-between style of exorcism—neither black nor white magic. It could be called "silver magic." When audiences shiver at something up there on the screen, chances are that it never happened on the set. There are countless instances of performances that were maneuvered through editing, coaxed out of different stars through psychological ruses, or just invented by directors in a flash of cinematographic intuition.

Directors guard their tricks of the trade with the jealousy of professional magicians. Any leak of the truth may kill the effect. Young Linda Blair lost a supporting Oscar for *The Exorcist* because too much was revealed about how William Friedkin pieced her performance together. Blair's double informed the press that she had played the levitation scenes. Mercedes McCambridge demanded a credit for dubbing the demon's voice. Then Friedkin counterattacked by saying that those chilling growls had been achieved by mixing several tracks that included not only Miss Blair and Miss McCambridge's voices, but also animal shrieks and, in one instance, even the director's own voice. Despite Friedkin's impassioned defense, the illusion was irreparably destroyed.

Yet the assemblage of a performance—when not so blatantly mechanical or so blaringly trumpeted—can create stunning mirages of screen acting. A director with complete editing control can go through countless takes, scanning the gold and discarding the dross through the sieve of a well-adjusted Movieola. A patient, sympathetic director can make all the difference in the cutting room, especially when he is handling a "pure" movie star with no stage experience of sustaining emotions during long scenes.

132

Robert Walker's death scene in STRANGERS ON A TRAIN (1951), used again in MY SON JOHN (1952). At right: Farley Granger

CAT ON A HOT TIN ROOF (1958). With Paul Newman and Elizabeth Taylor

Elizabeth Taylor is excellent in *Cat on a Hot Tin Roof,* but watch the performance closely. The actress has a childlike, fleeting concentration; every time she is about to lose her intensity, director Richard Brooks cuts away from her face and gives her respite by focusing on the target of her tirade. Marilyn Monroe has never been as poignant as in *Bus Stop,* because Joshua Logan knew how far she could go and stopped each take within an inch of unconvincing disaster.

These are cliff-hanger performances, with the director as the stalwart hero who prevents the fall in the twenty-fourth fraction of a minute; a frame away from disintegration. George Cukor is a past master at this game. He has the eye of a hawk, the parsimony of a Scotsman. Cukor knew how far he could push Harlow, Crawford and Shearer in the thirties, but he was never as delicate as with Audrey Hepburn in *My Fair Lady.* The actress is in obvious trouble when she tries to convey the guttersnipe bravado of Eliza Doolittle in the first half. A swan by nature. Hepburn was striving desperately for the coarseness of the ugly duckling. Whenever she cannot cope with the grimy cheeks, the lopsided wig and the battered hat, Cukor discreetly cuts to Rex Harrison's reaction shots. Harrison looks so

appalled at her bedraggled appearance that the audience begins to believe in it—almost. It is a shrewd ploy to mark time until the second half, when Hepburn can turn from an unconvincing caterpillar into a glorious butterfly.

Silver magic can polish a star, but it can work both ways. There are endless case histories of actors who accused their directors of sabotaging their performances by deliberately choosing the worst take. But however vehemently the stars may protest, in most cases the destruction of a performance is not conceived in venom but in a misguided desire for the wrong effect. John Cassavetes claims that when he directed Judy Garland in *A Child is Waiting,* he was fully aware that she was prone to excess; he strictly restrained her for a couple of takes and then let her quiver and sob to her heart's content for a supernumerary take he had no intention of using. His work was then pre-empted by the boss: when producer Stanley Kramer saw Cassavetes' final cut, he thought the performance was cold and dry, not at all what the fans expected from four-handkerchief Garland. Kramer reinstated the weepy takes that the director had shot only to humor his high-strung star. The decision ruined not only her performance, but a very promising movie.

Judy Garland in A CHILD IS WAITING (1963)

Ingrid Bergman's moment of decision in CASABLANCA (1942), with Paul Henreid and Humphrey Bogart

A film director, by the nature of his craft, is a puppeteer who can make a person or a personality look better or worse, whichever way he pulls the strings. To choose a movie metaphor, he can be like Gepetto, Pinocchio's benign father, or like Stromboli, Pinocchio's malignant captor on Pleasure Island. When the director pulls the wrong string, there is catastrophe. When he pulls the right one, legends are born.

The camera has a quick, penetrating eye that pierces all fakery. Searching for a breath of spontaneity, sometimes directors pull a fast one with the adroitness of a flim-flam man. *A Man and a Woman*, Claude Lelouch's Oscar-winning film, is a case in point. The screenplay ended with the woman, Anouk Aimée, wandering along a railroad station after forsaking her lover, played by Jean-Louis Trintignant. The night before the scene was to be shot, Lelouch had a brainstorm. A happy ending was mandatory for this ultraromantic film or the audience would walk out of it teased and dejected.

Anouk Aimée was not informed of the change in plans. As the cameras rolled, she paced mournfully down the train station, like Anna Karenina before the fatal jump. Then, from the crowd of passersby, Trintignant suddenly emerged. He hugged her passionately. The actress was baffled but kept her composure and did not cry "What's going on here?". This was the final shot of the film. It won Anouk Aimée an Oscar nomination for that unforgettable look of wonder as she realized that her lover had

come back. In reality, the actress was just surprised to find out that Lelouch had rewritten the ending behind her back.

Director Michael Curtiz kept Ingrid Bergman in a similar state of uncertainty all through the filming of *Casablanca.* The script was being written page by page as they rushed the movie to completion. When Bergman asked Curtiz for direction, he could not specify which way her sentimental compass should point. Bergman insisted. Did she love her idealistic husband or the cynical casino owner? Curtiz had no idea how the movie would end, so he instructed Berman to "play it both ways" with Paul Henreid and Humphrey Bogart. As she wavered between both men, her indecision spiked the film like a shot of vodka in a glass of orange juice. Curtiz saw the rushes, realized what was happening and wisely remained silent. Even when the final pages were delivered, he did not tell Bergman which of the two characters she was supposed to favor. The disorientation worked so well that a slick programmer turned into a tantalizing classic.

Curtiz was an artisan who thought that movies, after all, were a form of "canned art." If the ingredients were not fresh to begin with, they might become poisoned with artifice by the time the product reached the screen. Directors have often preserved that precious spontaneity by not letting actors know exactly what they are doing. When William Wyler tested the novice Audrey Hepburn for *Roman Holiday,* he knew this slender reed of a girl had

Audrey Hepburn in ROMAN HOLIDAY (1953)

Jean-Pierre Léaud in THE 400 BLOWS (1959)

the deceptive strength to pinion his movie fable. If only she would loosen up and let the camera catch her unaware....

For the screen test, Wyler had her waking up in a regal bed, playing the role of an unruly princess. She delivered her lines with the stiffness of an amateur, but then Wyler said "Cut" and kept the cameras rolling. As soon as the ordeal was over, Hepburn relaxed, clapped her hands and asked "Was I any good?" Wyler used this bit of unrehearsed charm to get cautious Paramount to sign her. The test was later shown on television as part of Hepburn's promotion for the film. Shots of it were printed in a publicity spread in *Life* magazine. Most important of all, Wyler ran the test frequently for Hepburn, until she was able to recreate that breathless enchantment all through the film, and win an Oscar for it.

Another cleverly utilized screen test certified the triumph of François Truffaut's first movie, *The 400 Blows*. Truffaut was interviewing dozens of children for the part of the lonely, rebellious boy. One day, an exceptionally bright twelve-year-old, Jean-Pierre Léaud—the son of actress Jacqueline Pierreux—was brought by his mother to Truffaut, to be tested for the role of Antoine Doinel. Truffaut insisted on talking to the child alone. The boy opened up to every indiscreet question the director asked about his family life, his inner feelings, his budding sexual appetites.

Young Léaud had no idea that a camera, hidden behind a bookcase, was recording his very candid replies. When Truffaut screened the result, he was enchanted with the child and instantly gave Léaud the part of Doinel. The film was quasi-autobiographical and Truffaut had found the perfect alter ego for this frank revelation of his own adolescent years. Truffaut also inserted the test as part of the picture: it was presented as an interview by an unseen psychologist who drills the child in a correctional institution. Truffaut substituted his own questioning voice for that of an off-screen woman who "played" the inquisitor. The sequence was choppily edited with gaps in the continuity covered up by disconcerting fadeouts. They were simply a technical ruse to eliminate some of Léaud's shocking answers, the ones that would never have escaped the strictures of the censors or the anger of the boy's parents. This five-minute interlude was widely praised by the critics and cemented Léaud's career as a very active performer in French films. It remains the most affecting "scene" in *The 400 Blows*. But in calling it a "scene," quotation marks are advisable.

Child actors, of course, are putty in the hands of directors who invade their fantasy world. Margaret O'Brien would huddle with her mother in a corner of the set, where she would be told a sad story that put her in the mood for a very effective crying jag. Directors soon were on to the trick and Vincente Minnelli has admitted that one of her finest moments of distress in *Meet Me in St.*

Louis—her hysterical destruction of the snowmen in the yard—erupted after he informed her that her puppy was going to be killed.

According to many directors, all actors are like children. Yet it is far more dangerous to play games with ego-puffed adults. Michael Curtiz, one of the legendary Hollywood tyrants, was able to become a grumpy surrogate parent to no less an imposing star than Joan Crawford. The pampered MGM goddess had fallen on hard times and had to start all over at Warners in *Mildred Pierce*. The first day on the set, Curtiz turned into the disapproving sire. He slashed the prominent shoulder pads from her dress and asked Crawford to wash all that lipstick from her garish, rectangular mouth. A resentful, chastened Crawford complied. With a martyred look, she suffered and suffered as a cowed, sacrificial mother. The performance garnered her an Academy Award, but she would never work with Curtiz again.

A director can approach his subject from the opposite angle and play not the stern but the permissive parent. Joan Fontaine has never been as spirited and as lovely as in *Frenchman's Creek,* because director Mitchell Leisen sensed how insecure she was and instructed everyone to tell Fontaine how beautiful she looked each morning as she walked on the set. Leisen also knew the actress was overly conscientious and had a tendency to embroider her roles. The first take was usually perfect, but Fontaine insisted on elaborating, thus marring the initial impact.

Leisen would let her go on, sometimes with no film on the camera, until she was pleased with her own effort and ready to tackle the next scene. She was confident that she had done herself proud with Take Seven, when only Take One existed, ready for printing.

As in all filial relationships, the balance is usually tipped by patience on both sides. But there are no set rules. Alfred Hitchcock is too impatient to play either stern or complacent father all through a film. "Actors are cattle," he said in the forties. In the intervening decades, he learned to shepherd them with imperturbable calm. When a blocked Joan Fontaine could not dissolve into tears in *Rebecca*, he did not coddle her like Leisen later would, but requested her permission and then slapped her into action. While shooting *Suspicion*, Fontaine could not summon the look of surprise and horror Hitchcock needed for a close-up, so he persuaded co-star Cary Grant to give her a nudge. As the cameras rolled, Grant stood next to Fontaine and berated her in the rudest manner. She gasped incredulously at this unwarranted attack. Hitchcock blithely shouted "Cut!" and the day's schedule proceeded without further delay. Fontaine was soothed from her shock by a bottle of vintage champagne in her dressing room and an eventual Oscar for her performance.

Hitchcock was not as persuasive when he directed Kim Novak in *Vertigo*. She claimed he treated her like an object, which was indeed what she was in the screenplay.

MILDRED PIERCE (1945). With Jack Carson and Joan Crawford

Greta Garbo in QUEEN CHRISTINA (1933)

As Madeleine, she played a woman invented out of dyed hair, tailored suits and inscrutable countenance to fit James Stewart's necrophiliac obsession. "I wanted her face to be blank, but she insisted on doodling on it," Hitchcock said. Failing to restrain her on the set, he just edited all the "doodles" out in the Movieola. Novak's ghostly, impassive, hypnotic performance is at once her best and the one she hates the most.

Still another trick had to be played when Hitchcock directed Montgomery Clift in *I Confess*. The film was precut in the director's mind. As usual in Hitchcock thrillers, when an actor looks towards the left, the audience can be sure some sort of menace will be coming from that angle. Clift refused to be a puppet in this visual ballet. His gaze would shift to the right, his eyes would flutter up or down, following the unpredictable rudder of his inner motivations. When Hitchcock realized he could not politely escort Clift into a maze of rigged intercutting, he wasted no time in arguments and went back

to the Kuleshov *montage* primer. Clift's close-ups were shot first, just like Ivan Mousjoukine's. Then the matching scenes were rearranged to dovetail with the actor's idiosyncracies, turning each blank look into a reaction shot. Clift thought he had had the upper hand, but by reversing the scheme Hitchcock, the master puppeteer, had stealthily trapped him into obedience.

Novak and Clift staged their fight for individuality on the set, but both were cut down to size in the editing room. The process is not as easy when editing is out of the question because the director must sustain the actor's expression in a long, silent, climactic sequence in which any break in continuity would be fatal to the mood. In such circumstances, the Kuleshov method does not apply and only friendly persuasion works. For the ending of *Queen Christina*, Garbo stood at the prow of her ship, sailing into exile with John Gilbert's dead body at her side. Director Rouben Mamoulian wanted the camera to explore Garbo's face for several minutes, but the actress was restless. She kept falling back into mannerisms—the raised eyebrow, the drooping eyelid, the delicious bite of the lower lip. Finally Mamoulian advised her to keep her face a blank and think of absolutely nothing for three minutes. Garbo obeyed and her face became a mirror into which every emotion could be read by the audience: sorrow, determination, regret, spiritual release, alternating on a shining surface.

For one indelible moment, Mamoulian played Svengali to Garbo's Trilby. But the Svengali-Trilby relationship has often escalated into full-fledged mental possession of the star by the director. Marlon Brando admitted he was having "woman trouble" during the filming of *On the Waterfront* and Elia Kazan, finding a chink in his tough armor, badgered him into giving a great performance, and also into a staunch refusal to work with his mentor ever again. Kazan did the same thing with Andy Griffith in *A Face in the Crowd*. Griffith was an easygoing, sweet-tempered performer who had made his fortune as a lov-

able bumbler in the stage version of *No Time for Sergeants*. Kazan needled him into frenzy and created Lonesome Rhoades, a Frankenstein monster, yokel style. It was the high point of Griffith's dramatic career but he confessed that Kazan had driven him to the point of punching walls and frothing at the mouth. After the experience, he preferred to settle down in profitable, long-running and peaceful television series.

Getting under the actor's skin often involves painful surgery, but all this Stanislavskian trauma must seem baffling to a self-confessed film puppeteer like Federico Fellini. The actors very seldom have access to the screenplay of his movies and in many scenes they have only the vaguest idea of what is going on. Since no definite dialogue has been written, players move around the set muttering numbers. "One, two, three, four," they say, not knowing what lines are eventually going to be dubbed in the soundtrack during the final mixing. The end result is anybody's guess and sometimes torment: for *La Dolce*

A FACE IN THE CROWD (1957). With Andy Griffith and Patricia Neal

Vita, Fellini persuaded members of the Italian nobility to walk around elegantly in a party sequence that ended up as a prelude to an orgy. At the opening night of the film in Milan, an outraged countess slapped Fellini and an irate prince spat on him.

Even more disquieting things can happen when Luis Buñuel is at the helm. Shooting *Viridiana* in Spain, under strict censorship, Buñuel staged a sequence in which a group of beggars invade the heroine's ancestral home. The ruffians sat down to a noisy dinner and Buñuel was exquisitely careful of how their profiles were turned to the camera and how each hand or even finger was raised. When the film was finished, he took the footage to be edited in France. He stopped the banquet scene in a freeze frame and his purpose became clear: he had placed the figures to create an exact parody of Leonardo Da Vinci's *The Last Supper*. The thirteen actors had had no idea that they had been trapped into blasphemy by Buñuel, the irredeemable anticlerical prankster.

Such awesome power cannot be escaped; it is inherent to the medium. On film, anything can happen. With such hazards facing them, it is no wonder that actors scamper back to the relative safety of the theatre or join the enemy by becoming directors or producers: their own puppeteers. Those in between must accept the fact that anyone who stands in front of a movie camera is guilty of an indiscretion. And that is perhaps why the wisest words ever uttered in a movie set came from a highly unlikely sage: Victor Mature. Just before a crucial close-up in *The Sharkfighters*, Mature turned to director Jerry Hopper and moaned the definitive plea of the beleaguered star against his inscrutable manipulator: "Make me look good, Jerry, but if you can't make me look good, make me look innocent."

LA DOLCE VITA (1960). With Marcello Mastroianni and Anita Ekberg

GENTLEMAN RAOUL

By Jeanine Basinger

Like everybody else in the United States who is my age, I spent my youth at the movies. Although names and faces of teachers and playmates from those days grow dimmer with each passing year, the movie memories stay sharp and clear—honed by repeated adult viewings, to be sure, but still imbued with their initial impact. In my mind, real events and vicarious film experiences are happily wed: a cold January Sunday afternoon when I passed up Carlene Hansen's ice-skating party to sit through two viewings of *The Big Sleep*. The hot summer when I braved the doctor's warnings about mixing in crowds (the polio scare kept small children away from swimming pools and movies) to sneak in to see *To Each His Own*, wearing my handkerchief tied over my nose to ward off the germs. The birthday celebration that took fifteen giggling little girls to Nick's Hamburger Shop for "all we could eat," followed by Betty Grable and June Haver in *The Dolly Sisters*.

We appreciated the movies for the stories they told and the stars who were in them. In those days nobody thought much about film directors. We all knew about Frank Capra and Alfred Hitchcock, and we had heard of John Ford and Elia Kazan. But we never talked about *them*. We talked about Joan Crawford, with her mink and her revolver, and about Errol Flynn's winning the war in Burma. We thought about the scares and the laughs we got from the movies that played our small town.

As we grew older, inevitably, some of us became buffs and began to memorize movie credits. And when I entered high school and started working as an usher in the local moviehouse, I not only memorized credits but often filled the boring hours of repeated viewings with little games which became a kind of film study. Counting the number of "blinks" (I didn't know about cuts then) in a film. Watching the audience to see how long the movie had been running before someone got bored and went to the candy counter. Watching a film *only* for the camera movement instead of the plot. And, sometimes, seeing how many other films I could name that had the same star . . . or character actor . . . or designer . . . or producer . . . or cinematographer . . . or, finally, director. High on my list of directors whose name on the screen

meant that no one went to the candy counter, that the camera moved, that there really would be some action was—Raoul Walsh.

A Walsh film was always good entertainment. Repeated viewings of his films also opened up deeper feelings of tenderness and human respect amidst the more noticeable rowdyisms of his masculine-oriented action pictures. I saw every film that came to town during the fifties, and none wore better than the pictures of Raoul Walsh. Of course, my opinions were seldom shared by the moviegoing townspeople. In those days, art was defined as anything alien and difficult to understand. Those were the years in which a "serious" American movie was directed by Elia Kazan or William Wyler, and was preferably based on a Broadway play. If a film came from Europe, it was automatically considered better than anything out of Hollywood, and if nobody understood it, it was probably a masterpiece. Movies like *A Lion is in the Streets*, *Battle Cry*, *The Tall Men*, and even *Band of Angels* ("You like a movie with Yvonne DeCarlo?" friends moaned) were overlooked, while awestruck audiences sat through films where misunderstood young men smashed their fists through plate-glass windows. Now that was serious stuff. (After all, in the Midwest, you could get arrested if you did that very often!)

Nevertheless, I went right on loving Raoul Walsh movies and I treasured his name, which seemed dashing and romantic, like his films.

I found out later that many of the movies my friends and I had loved as small children had also been directed by Walsh: *Objective Burma*, *White Heat*, *Along the Great Divide*, *Pursued*. It was only natural that after I began teaching American film history, one of the courses I would set up, working on the "auteur theory," would be based on the films "by Raoul Walsh." I had the pleasure of introducing my students to many of my favorite films from the past . . . and also, through my friends at the Yale Law School Film Society (Bob Bookman and Peter Broderick), of introducing them to the man himself, Gentleman Raoul, as they later dubbed him.

When I first announced that the director whose work we had been studying (and loving) all semester would visit our class, my students were naturally thrilled and

143

ME AND MY GAL (1932). With Joan Bennett and Spencer Tracy.

excited. And curious, as I had once been. What would Raoul Walsh be like in person? How old was he, and what did he look like? The celebration of Walsh as a great American film-maker (despite the best auteurist efforts) was still a relatively new thing. The celebration of Raoul Walsh the man as a great personality was still in the future. Remembering my own curiosity, I asked the class —what would you expect Walsh to be like, based on his movies?

Their answers naturally reflected their filmic sense of the man who had directed the free-wheeling *Gentleman Jim*, the hilarious and rowdy *Me and My Gal*, the downright irreverent and vulgar *Bowery*, the tough-minded *High Sierra*, and the warmly human *Strawberry Blonde*. My class well knew how they thought "the only director who could have gotten away with a shot of James Cagney sitting on his mother's lap" *ought* to look.

Maybe he would wear cowboy boots and a ten-gallon hat—and a loud sports jacket of some unusual plaid. Maybe he would have a red bandanna around his neck. They pictured a man who would tell colorful, even off-

color stories while hand-rolling a cigarette. Perhaps, they speculated wildly, he would wear an eye-patch like director Nicholas Ray, who had been on campus the previous year. Maybe—oh, joy!—he would turn out to be an authentic American primitive, one of the tall men in person.

When, following a much-appreciated screening of Walsh's *Baby Face Harrington*, I walked into the theatre with a man wearing a loud sports jacket, a flowered red bandanna, a ten-gallon hat, high-heeled cowboy boots— and a black eye-patch set rakishly over one eye—I'm sure they thought I had sent over to Central Casting for an "old-time film director type" to bamboozle a class of greenhorns. When this colorful creature turned out to be none other than Raoul Walsh for real and in person, their delight was reflected in their boisterous applause. When Walsh also turned out to be a raconteur of the first order, telling hilarious story after hilarious story, acting out characters and recalling events as if they were yesterday—their joy was uncontained. It was one of those perfect moments when the right class met the right director at the right time. All the stories were new and un-

144

published—all the fun was in the discovery.

At first, it was all seriousness. "How," asked one earnest young film-maker, "did you make the transition to sound from your days as a silent-film director?" "That reminds me of a story," answered Walsh, and he was off, telling how he had originally intended to be the star of *In Old Arizona* (an early sound-location film, for which he was co-director), but an automobile accident had cost him his eye, ending his career as an actor. ("You'd be surprised how few roles there are for one-eyed cowboys," he commented wryly.)

"How," asked another hopeful, "did you handle the direction of the song-and-dance numbers in the musicals you made?"

"Well," drawled Walsh, hand-rolling a cigarette, "I had a foolproof system. I just went outside and had a smoke until they were all finished with the damned things."

"Were you ever hampered by censorship?"

"Hell, no. I just put in one reel that would make the censor's dandruff dance. He'd be so busy throwing that reel out, he'd miss all the rest of the stuff."

"Could you comment on Andrew Sarris' description of a typical Walsh hero as more interested in what he's doing than in the why and how of it?"

"No, I couldn't comment . . . what the hell, maybe Sarris was drunk when he said it."

After a few minutes of this, the more scholarly members of the class knew when they were licked. We settled down to a wonderful session in which, if the in-depth information about "the creation of the cinema" was in short order, who cared? Walsh's stories, as told by him, were a lot more enjoyable than any aesthetic ramblings, and somehow more appropriate, too. We heard all about a drunken weekend he had shared with John Barrymore. ("That guy never took a bath—he smelled like a monkey's wedding.") About how he had met Pancho Villa face-to-face ("I just kept talking and talking, but I sure as hell kept one eye on the door.")

He treated us to his opinions on James Cagney ("a nice guy, but he ate too much"), and George Raft ("Georgie wouldn't know a good script if it fell on his head"),

GENTLEMAN JIM (1942). With Sammy Stein and Errol Flynn

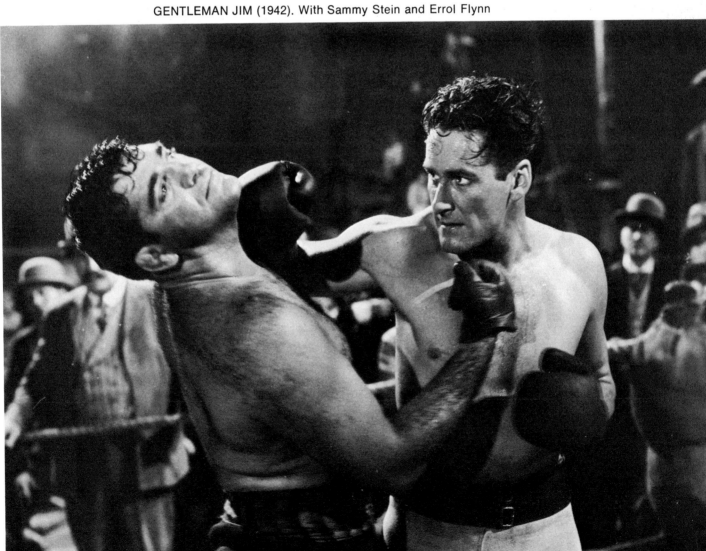

OBJECTIVE BURMA (1944). Errol Flynn leads his men into battle.

to Ann Sheridan ("a beautiful girl") to Virginia Mayo ("a beautiful girl") to Ida Lupino ("a beautiful girl . . . but she was tough").

Asked what his relationships with his leading ladies had been, Walsh slyly asked, "Off-screen or on?" When pressed by a dedicated women's liberationist for his attitudes on the woman's role in his male-oriented world, Walsh shrewdly sized up the attitude of women stars toward working in his films. "Well, look. Actresses were sometimes unhappy in my films. And why not? I made a lot of action pictures, with rough location work, where the story was about men and their brave deeds. The actress would be seen at the beginning of the film, holding a half-inch of knitting, waving good-bye to the hero. Then she'd be seen again in the last ten minutes, with two feet of knitting, waving hello. There's not a hell of a lot of Oscars given out for knitting."

Besides the Hollywood stories, he told about his sewing up a wounded cowboy in Montana (because the doctor was too drunk to do it), and offered vivid memories of parties at San Simeon . . . and plenty more. The highlight for tall stories occurred when one of my students (who had read the anecdote in Errol Flynn's autobiography) asked if it were true that Walsh had taken the dead body of John Barrymore up to Errol Flynn's house as a grisly joke on the drunk Flynn. At first reluctant to tell it, but warming to the audience reaction, Walsh launched into the complete story, lacing it with appropriately humorous and macabre details.

According to the story (which has grown better with each telling since), Flynn, sorrowing over the death of his drinking buddy and idol, had availed himself of the occasion to get roaring drunk. "If only I could just see old Jack again, just once, sitting right there in that

WHITE HEAT (1949). With Edmond O'Brien, James Cagney, and Virginia Mayo.

Raoul Walsh on the set of BLACKBEARD THE PIRATE (1952) with Linda Darnell

chair," Flynn had sobbed to Walsh, "I'd give anything. Why, I'd give a million dollars and my best address book."

Raoul Walsh was not a man to let a friend down. Within no time, while Flynn slept it off, he was off to the mortuary to "borrow" Barrymore's body—which he suitably arranged in the very chair Flynn had indicated. Walsh's imitation of Flynn finding the body brought the house down! And as if that weren't enough, Walsh added that he did not take Flynn up on the offer of a million dollars. (We were left in the dark about the address book, however.) Topping his own story with the final touch, Walsh calmly added that when he returned Barrymore's body and told the mortuary attendant what he had done, that good man (apparently calm of mien where dead bodies were concerned) said, "Well, hell, if you'd told me where you were taking him, I'd have put a better suit on him."

Afterwards, we had a small reception, and the stories went on and on. When it was finally time to leave, a spontaneous standing ovation took place—to which Walsh bowed, doffed his cowboy hat, and—just as he was leaving the room—quickly pulled out a pair of imaginary six-guns and "shot" into the air.

Walking to the car, he said to me, "Well, do you think they liked it?" I told him gravely that, yes, I rather thought they did. We had our pictures taken together in the parking lot, and before he drove off, he leaned out of the car window and said to me, "I feel sorry for Jack [Ford]. I hear he's in the hospital now. I hope I can just keep going and going. When they come to honor me, if they ever do, I'm comin' in on a horse."

Later, after four intense days of applause at a Yale film retrospective, Walsh (accompanied by Bob Bookman) went to the airport to board the plane for Los Angeles. Bob reported later that he himself was worn out, but Walsh was going strong. With thirty minutes until plane time, Bob sank exhausted into a lounge chair. "That's right," Walsh had told him, "you take a rest. I'm just going to nose around here and look over the action."

And with that, the man old enough to be not only Bob's father, but his grandfather (even his great-grandfather!) trotted off to look over the airport sights. Whatever action there was, no doubt it couldn't hold a candle to Gentleman Raoul. Whatever happens, wherever he may be, Raoul Walsh will always be "comin' in on a horse!" Long may he live!

THE DIRECTOR'S CHAIR (I):

Here is a quiz built around the work of five of Hollywood's leading directors. Score four points for each correct answer.

I. Alfred Hitchcock

A. In which film did Hitchcock appear as the portly "before" figure in a "before/after" diet ad in a newspaper?

B. *The Lady Vanishes* was Hitchcock's 1938 classic melodrama. Who played the vanished lady?

C. Hitchcock speaking: "We started out with the idea of the windmill sequence and also the scene of the murderer escaping through the bobbing umbrellas." Which movie is he talking about?

D. In which film did Claude Rains say, "Mother, I am married to an American agent."

E. A bearded lady. A blind old man. Which Hitchcock movie do they evoke?

II. John Ford

A. Mary Kate Danaher is the heroine of which John Ford film?

B. John Ford directed Katharine Hepburn in only one film. What was its name?

C. Jane Darwell gave an unforgettable performance as Ma Joad in Ford's *The Grapes of Wrath*. But who played *Pa* Joad? Was it Henry Hull, Charley Grapewin, Russell Simpson, or Walter Brennan?

D. *Mister Roberts* marked the last screen performance of which stalwart actor?

E. Who played the title role in Ford's *The Man Who Shot Liberty Valance*?

III. William Wyler

A. "Are you afraid, Mama?" is a key line of which Wyler movie?

B. A red ballroom gown. Yellow fever. Which Wyler film do they evoke?

C. William Wyler directed Audrey Hepburn in two films. One was her Award-winning American debut in *Roman Holiday*. What was the second? (Hint: he had directed an altered version of the same story twenty-six years earlier.)

D. This Wyler-directed film won six Academy Awards, including one for an actor who never made another film. What was the film and who was the actor?

E. Wyler directed Humphrey Bogart in two films. In both, Bogart played an unsavory killer. What are the names of the films?

IV. Cecil B. DeMille

A. "This is one kiss you won't be able to wipe off." In which DeMille movie is this line spoken, and by whom?

B. A giant squid furnishes the climax of which DeMille extravaganza?

C. DeMille's last film was *The Greatest Show on Earth* in 1952, about the circus. Who played the part of the famous clown, Emmett Kelly?

D. Who played the Indian chieftain in the 1947 film, *Unconquered*? Another distinguished actor played an Indian chieftain in DeMille's *North West Mounted Police* in 1940. His name?

E. In 1932 she bathed in asses' milk for DeMille. Two years later, also for DeMille, she seduced Marc Antony. Her name?

V. George Cukor

A. "My, she was y'ar," is a well-remembered line from which Cukor movie?

B. Who played the title role in Cukor's *Edward My Son* (1949)?

C. One of Cukor's best films, *The Marrying Kind* (1952) introduced a new young actor. His name?

D. George Cukor directed Katharine Hepburn in her first film, then went on to direct her in seven more films over a number of years. What was the title of the first film?

E. Cukor directed Garbo in her last film, *Two-Faced Woman* (1942). In this disastrous film, who stole the show (or what little was worth stealing), playing Melvyn Douglas' ex-girlfriend, Griselda Vaughan?

(Answers on page 190)

THE DIRECTOR'S CHAIR (II):

For this second quiz about directors, you are asked, in each case, to name the film *not* directed by the person cited (for four points each).

1. Frank Capra: *American Madness, Magic Town, Here Comes the Groom, Broadway Bill.*

2. Fred Zinnemann: *Act of Violence, Oklahoma!, The Valley of Decision, The Sundowners.*

3. George Seaton: *Mr. 880, The Proud and the Profane, For Heaven's Sake, The Hook.*

4. Rouben Mamoulian: *The Mark of Zorro, The Gay Desperado, Yolanda and the Thief, Summer Holiday.*

5. Howard Hawks: *Ceiling Zero, Only Angels Have Wings, Air Force, Dive Bomber.*

6. Fritz Lang: *The Long Night, The Secret Beyond the Door, The Return of Frank James, While the City Sleeps.*

7. Elia Kazan: *Wild River, No Way Out, Sea of Grass, Pinky.*

8. Michael Curtiz: *Mission to Moscow, Janie, Roughly Speaking, Mr. Skeffington.*

9. Delmer Daves: *Hollywood Canteen, Rome Adventure, Christmas in Connecticut, 3:10 to Yuma.*

10. Otto Preminger: *Forever Amber, Daisy Kenyon, Angel Face, Claudia and David.*

Continued

The Director's Chair: Howard Hawks filming RED RIVER (1948) with John Wayne

11. Leo McCarey: *Duck Soup, Good Sam, Sing, You Sinners, My Favorite Wife.*
12. Mervyn LeRoy: *Boy Meets Girl, Three Men on a Horse, In the Good Old Summertime, Lovely to Look At.*
13. W. S. Van Dyke: *The Thin Man, After the Thin Man, Another Thin Man, The Thin Man Goes Home.*
14. William Dieterle: *A Dispatch From Reuters, The Searching Wind, Edge of Darkness, Love Letters.*
15. Josef von Sternberg: *The King Steps Out, Sundown, Sergeant Madden, Macao.*
16. Vincente Minnelli: *Kismet, Brigadoon, Silk Stockings, Bells Are Ringing.*
17. David Lean: *This Happy Breed, One Woman's Story, Quartet, Hobson's Choice.*
18. Joseph M. Mankiewicz: *Come to the Stable, Five Fingers, House of Strangers, The Late George Apley.*
19. Lewis Milestone: *The General Died at Dawn, The Purple Heart, The Moon Is Down, Pork Chop Hill.*
20. Billy Wilder: *Five Graves to Cairo, Spirit of St. Louis, The Mating Season, Kiss Me, Stupid.*
21. Henry Hathaway: *The Lives of a Bengal Lancer, The House on 92nd Street, Niagara, The Tall Men.*
22. King Vidor: *Street Scene, The Texas Rangers, Lightning Strikes Twice, Five Branded Women.*
23. Lloyd Bacon: *Marked Woman, Dodge City, Action in the North Atlantic, I Wonder Who's Kissing Her Now.*
24. George Stevens: *Vivacious Lady, The More the Merrier, To Each His Own, The Stalking Moon.*
25. Alan Dwan: *Curly Top, Getting Gertie's Garter, Sands of Iwo Jima, Cattle Queen of Montana.*

(*Answers on page 190*)

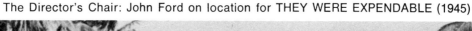

The Director's Chair: John Ford on location for THEY WERE EXPENDABLE (1945)

THERE'S NO BUSINESS LIKE SHOW BUSINESS (1953). With Johnnie Ray, Mitzi Gaynor, Dan Dailey, Ethel Merman, Donald O'Connor, and Marilyn Monroe

THE MOVIE SONGSMITHS

Here is a quiz centering on the songwriters who have contributed their music to films over the years. Simply match the songwriter with his song and with the film in which the song appeared.

"Sure Thing"	George Gershwin	*Ziegfeld Follies*
"You Are Too Beautiful"	Hugh Martin	*We're Not Dressing*
"Too Late Now"	Jule Styne	*The Bandwagon*
"A Boy Chases a Girl"	Jimmy McHugh	*Going My Way*
"Young and Healthy"	Ralph Rainger	*Hans Christian Andersen*
"Things Are Looking Up"	Richard Rodgers	*A Date With Judy*
"You Stepped Out of a Dream"	Jerome Kern	*There's No Business Like Show Business*
"Honey in the Honeycomb"	Harry Warren	*Ziegfeld Girl*
"Love Thy Neighbor"	Burton Lane	*Cover Girl*
"This Heart of Mine"	Jimmy Van Heusen	*The Big Broadcast of 1938*
"I Fall In Love Too Easily"	Cole Porter	*42nd Street*
"Anywhere I Wander"	Irving Berlin	*Royal Wedding*
"The Day After Forever"	Harold Arlen	*The Pirate*
"Thanks For the Memory"	Frank Loesser	*Cabin in the Sky*
"You Can Do No Wrong"	Nacio Herb Brown	*A Damsel in Distress*
"I Guess I'll Have to Change My Plan"	Arthur Schwartz	*Anchors Aweigh*
"It's a Most Unusual Day"	Harry Revel	*Hallelujah, I'm a Bum*

(*Answers on page 191*)

UNHERALDED AND UNSUNG

This quiz concerns the many talented and imaginative people who work behind the cameras and out of the glamour spotlight: the producers, directors, writers, composers, photographers, art directors, etc.. Score four points for each correct answer, and a score over 80 rates a bow of thanks from the "unheralded and unsung" movie people.

1. Director Sam Wood did long-time duty at MGM and later at Warners, carrying out most of his assignments with professional ease. One of his best-known films is:
   a. *On Borrowed Time*
   b. *Goodbye, Mr. Chips*
   c. *Edison the Man*

2. In 1951 the Academy Award for the best scoring of a dramatic or comedy picture went to Franz Waxman for his score for:
   a. *A Place in the Sun*
   b. *Detective Story*
   c. *Death of a Salesman*

3. In 1965 the Academy Award for the best screenplay based on material from another medium went to Robert Bolt for:
   a. *Ship of Fools*
   b. *The Spy Who Came In From the Cold*
   c. *Dr. Zhivago*

4. Arthur Edeson is:
   a. a cinematographer who photographed *Casablanca*
   b. a prominent art director whose credits include *The African Queen*
   c. composer of many well-known musical scores, including *The Best Years of Our Lives*

5. The screenplay for Alfred Hitchcock's *Psycho* was written by:
   a. Robert Bloch
   b. Evan Hunter
   c. Joseph Stefano

6. The first Academy Award for direction went to:
   a. Josef von Sternberg for *The Last Command*
   b. William A. Wellman for *Wings*
   c. Frank Borzage for *Seventh Heaven*

7. Cedric Gibbons was:
   a. Dance director at Fox during the forties
   b. MGM's art director for many years
   c. One of the founders of the Technicolor process

8. Which of the following movies is *not* a David O. Selznick production?
   a. *The Adventures of Tom Sawyer*
   b. *I'll Be Seeing You*
   c. *The Bishop's Wife*

9. Among the films he directed are *All This and Heaven, Too, Blues in the Night, The Snake Pit,* and *Anastasia.* His name is:
   a. Michael Curtiz
   b. Anatole Litvak
   c. William Dieterle

10. Elmer Bernstein is:
   a. a composer of many film scores
   b. award-winning photographer for *Citizen Kane* and other films
   c. head of the Special Effects Department at Paramount since the fifties

11. For which of these films did George Gershwin *not* write the score?
   a. *The Goldwyn Follies*
   b. *The Shocking Miss Pilgrim*
   c. *Centennial Summer*

12. Which of the following films was *not* directed by Cecil B. DeMille?
   a. *Four Frightened People*
   b. *Solomon and Sheba*
   c. *The Plainsman*

13. He acted in Chaplin short films, then later directed such movies as *Boy Meets Girl* and *A Slight Case of Murder.* His name is:
   a. William Keighley
   b. Lloyd Bacon
   c. Vincent Sherman

14. John Ford's last film with John Wayne was:
   a. *Donovan's Reef*
   b. *How the West Was Won*
   c. *The Man Who Shot Liberty Valance*

15. *Too Many Husbands*, *The Hour Before the Dawn*, and *The Seventh Sin* were all based on stories by:
   a. Edna Ferber
   b. W. Somerset Maugham
   c. A. J. Cronin

16. Casey Robinson was:
   a. composer for many Paramount musicals in the thirties
   b. a busy screenwriter for Warners in the thirties and forties
   c. director of many Universal action melodramas in the forties

17. Before turning to direction, Preston Sturges wrote many screenplays. Which of the following was written by Sturges?
   a. *Hands Across the Table*
   b. *The Gilded Lily*
   c. *Easy Living*

18. Which of the following plot lines does *not* come from a film produced by Samuel Goldwyn?
   a. A low-class but self-sacrificing mother watches her daughter's wedding from the outside.
   b. A blinded war veteran named Al Schmid tries to return to normal life, with great difficulty.
   c. A staid professor, carrying out his research into American slang, meets a flashy nightclub singer.

19. For the film version of *My Fair Lady*, the voice of Audrey Hepburn was dubbed by:
   a. Sally Ann Howes
   b. Florence Henderson
   c. Marni Nixon

20. In 1965 the Academy Award for the year's best song went to:
   a. "The Shadow of Your Smile," from *The Sandpiper*
   b. "My Favorite Things," from *The Sound of Music*
   c. "Hush . . . Hush, Sweet Charlotte," from the film of the same name

21. Miklos Rozsa composed the score for which one of the following films?
   a. *Ivanhoe*
   b. *Solomon and Sheba*
   c. *Spartacus*

22. The screenplays for *The Grapes of Wrath*, *The Woman in the Window*, and *We're Not Married* were all written by:
   a. Philip Dunne
   b. Moss Hart
   c. Nunnally Johnson

23. *Come Back, Little Sheba*, *The Last Angry Man*, and *Butterfield 8* were directed by:
   a. Delbert Mann
   b. Daniel Mann
   c. Anthony Mann

24. Dorothy Arzner is
   a. award-winning designer of the costumes for *Gigi*
   b. head of the makeup department at MGM for many years
   c. one of the few women directors in film history

25. For many years the adviser on all Technicolor films was:
   a. Helen Rose   b. Natalie Kalmus
   c. Virginia Van Upp

(Answers on page 191)

THE LAST ANGRY MAN (1959). With Joby Baker and Paul Muni (Who directed?)

HUD (1963). With Paul Newman and Melvyn Douglas. Photographed by James Wong Howe

JAMES WONG HOWE

By Nicholas Yanni

In 1911 in Pasco, Washington, a druggist named John Sullivan gave a twelve-year-old Chinese-American a Brownie camera for hauling four hundred empty beer bottles. That was probably the beginning of James Wong Howe's love affair with photography—and certainly American motion pictures are all the better for it. Approximately 125 movies later (stretching from Pola Negri to Elizabeth Taylor), Howe is generally recognized as one of the finest of Hollywood's cinematographers. A former prizefighter, he has applied the technique of the ring to his professional life: "You've got to move fast. You've got to use your noodle." And this is exactly what he has done.

Howe's job is not easy, especially when one considers the wide range of temperaments involved in the making of a movie. It involves the skillful co-ordination of the two basic elements—the players and the background, although it is generally admitted that most audiences are more interested in the former than the latter. Among the actresses—all great screen beauties—who have been flatteringly photographed by Howe are Marlene Dietrich, Vera Zorina, Myrna Loy, Norma Shearer, Clara Bow, Estelle Taylor, Bessie Love, Merle Oberon, Colleen Moore, Pola Negri, Gloria Swanson, Joan Crawford, and Loretta Young.

Howe's achievements in cinematography have been recognized by the Motion Picture Academy on many occasions—he received nominations for *Algiers* (1938), *Abe Lincoln in Illinois* (1940), *Kings Row* (1942), *Air Force* (1943), *The Rose Tattoo* (1955), *The Old Man and the Sea* (1958), *Hud* (1963), and *Seconds* (1966). He won awards for *The Rose Tattoo* and *Hud*.

Although he has contributed fully to Hollywood's image of soft-focus glamour, Howe has always excelled at photographing the realistic and even harsh aspects of life—his camera work in *Kings Row* greatly enhanced the sense of covert evil—and many well-remembered films bear the stamp of his skill at conveying unvarnished naturalism: the somber scientific milieu of William Dieterle's *Dr. Ehrlich's Magic Bullet* (1940); the grim war background of Fritz Lang's *Hangmen Also Die* (1942) or Raoul Walsh's *Objective Burma* (1944); the brutal boxing scene of Robert Rossen's *Body and Soul* (1947), with

some of the finest boxing photography ever achieved; the drab domestic setting of *Come Back, Little Sheba* (1952); and the shabby, vicious Broadway world of Alexander Mackendrick's *The Sweet Smell of Success* (1957). But Howe has also succeeded in expressing lyricism and nostalgia with his camera, as in Norman Taurog's *The Adventures of Tom Sawyer* (1938), Michael Curtiz's *Yankee Doodle Dandy* 1942), and Joshua Logan's *Picnic* (1955), where his photography was an important factor in capturing the lives of small-town Americans. Howe also directed two feature films, *Go, Man, Go* (1954) and *The Invisible Avenger* (1957), plus a short, *The World of Dong Kingman.**

Hollywood's only successful Chinese cameraman, Howe is a short, muscular man, with a flat nose and coal-black hair. Born in China in 1899 as Wong Tung Jim, Jimmy, as his friends call him, came to America at the age of five when his parents settled in a small railroad town in the state of Washington. Having been knocked out one time too many as a professional boxer, Howe entered the film business in 1917. He became a general handyman in the camera department at Famous Players-Lasky Studio, and during this period, he experimented with still photography, often taking pictures of actors in costume. It is said that the movie business originally interested him because an old-time boxing friend who himself had obtained a studio job told Howe of the "rosy" life a cameraman led (including the twelve-hour day and ten-dollars-a-week salary).

One day in 1922, Mary Miles Minter, a popular actress of the day, asked Howe to photograph her. She liked the stills so much (he managed to make her pale blue eyes look much darker than they really were) that she insisted the studio hire him as cameraman on her films. His first movie was *Drums of Fate*, with Miss Minter as a girl torn between an African explorer and a crippled musician.

The early years were not easy, however, and he was often plagued by racial discrimination and insults. He was

---

* In 1930, Howe produced, directed and photographed a Japanese film (title unknown), which was only shown in Japan, and in 1948 he began work in China on a film to be called *Rickshaw Boy*, but the project was abandoned. He wanted very much to direct MGM's large-scale production of Pearl Buck's *The Good Earth* in 1937, but Sidney Franklin won that assignment.

PICNIC (1955). Photographed by James Wong Howe

usually given the worst equipment on the lot, but when producers saw that he would turn out the best work, he was awarded a contract.

However, Howe almost shortened his career when he went to China during the advent of talking pictures. He was shooting backgrounds for a documentary which he had planned to direct himself about the farmers in that country. When he returned, producers claimed that he had no experience with the new sound films, and for a while he was unemployed. Finally, director William K. Howard gave Howe a chance to photograph his film *Transatlantic* in 1931. The picture was a great success, strengthened by Howe's imaginative photography. He created the claustrophobic feeling of life aboard ship by

insisting that the set designer put ceilings on the sets—it was a decade before Orson Welles did the same in *Citizen Kane*. (Howe also made early use of deep-focus photography for this picture.) His mobility with the camera demonstrated clearly that he had mastered the technique of the sound film.

In photographing Hollywood's most glamorous ladies over the years, Howe inevitably has a cluster of opinions and a scrapbook of memories. Curiously, he has said that the most beautiful of the silent-era actresses is one he never photographed: the "orchidaceous" Corinne Griffith. On one occasion, he wound up sleeping in Gloria Swanson's perfumed bed on the set of Cecil B. DeMille's *Male and Female*. (He put in many late hours for DeMille, and

158

often missed the last bus home, requiring him to sleep over at the studio.) Howe lit the close-ups for Hedy Lamarr's torrid love scene with Charles Boyer in *Algiers,* and afterwards the Hays office approved it. (He likes to think that they were probably "blinded" by Hedy Lamarr's beauty!)

Howe once spent three hours filming extreme close-ups of Greta Garbo at her request in a screen test for a projected comeback in a movie called *La Duchesse de Langeais,* to be produced in Italy by Walter Wanger with Max Ophuls as the director and James Mason as her co-star. Howe got the job because Garbo's old cameraman was ill. The movie was never made but Howe recalls being amazed that she did her own makeup and describes her as still "the most exciting face I have ever seen."

Based on the reports of the job he did for Garbo, Tallulah Bankhead insisted on Howe's working on John Cromwell's *Main Street to Broadway.* He remembers her telling the director: "Go ahead and do your worst—as long as that little so-and-so is behind the camera, I am not worried, dahling!"

Yet, after all these years, Howe has often admitted frankly that he has yet to see "a perfect face." "Gable's ears were too large; Dietrich's nose too wide, and Garbo needed proper lighting and makeup to come across."

Howe's ingenuity is well known in the industry. For example, in *Body and Soul,* he put himself on roller skates and used a small hand-held camera to shoot a dramatic fight sequence which captured the gritty realism of the boxing ring. The results are dazzling even today. In Robert Rossen's *The Brave Bulls* (1951), starring Mel Ferrer, Howe mounted a big bull's head on handlebars and had one of the matadors push it so as to create a close-up of a bull's head with just the horns coming by from the matador's point of view. Mel Ferrer never got near the bull!

At the end of *Picnic,* when the two lovers played by Kim Novak and William Holden part, apparently for good, Howe suggested to director Joshua Logan that they use an aerial shot that would pull back and show her train going one way and his bus going another—all in the same frame. This bold and imaginative shot was a great success, probably the most interesting in the film.

In *The Old Man and the Sea* (1958), Howe's extraordinary use of color was memorable; but few know that it was he who devised the manner by which a bird would come down on the hand of the old fisherman, played by Spencer Tracy—he weighted its feathers with BB shot!

If luck is involved with success in cinematography, it must be backed up by expertise and a talent for working smoothly with the director, for which Howe is well known. He has often said that when he differs with a director on how a scene should be shot, he usually shoots it twice—once his way, and once the director's—so that the director is then free to choose the "best" final version, which Howe, of course, hopes will be his.

The closeness of the cinematographer-director relationship while shooting a film is the reason Howe prefers working with the same director repeatedly in order to establish a rapport between them. Such was the case with Martin Ritt, for whom Howe did *Hud* (1963), *Outrage* (1964), *Hombre* (1967), and *The Molly Maguires* (1969). In *Hud,* shot in black-and-white and wide-screen, Howe matched the harsh, stinging story with his uncompromising and unforgettable West Texas landscapes. Howe shot Patricia Neal's face in a no-nonsense, unglamorous fashion (something he was not allowed to do with Myrna Loy in 1934 in *The Thin Man*). And in *The Molly Maguires,* a drama of coal mining in nineteenth-century Pennsylvania, he purposely gave the film a bleak look by subduing the costumes and sets and repainting everything in drab colors. (Howe wanted to shoot the film in black and white but was forced to do it in color because of the increased resale value to television.) As with his first color film, *The Adventures of Tom Sawyer,* Howe was faced with shooting *The Molly Maguires* in a cave-like surrounding. But unlike the cave sequence in *Tom Sawyer* (which employed candles as a focal light source), Howe was forced to make audiences believe that the only light came from the small oil lamp on the cap of each miner. Few, if any, cinematographers had ever risked shooting important scenes in such minimum of light —but Howe succeeded by attaching several high-intensity lamps to actors not facing the camera to provide enough light for the mine scenes.

This is one of the basic approaches to Howe's *realistic* approach to filmmaking techniques—known as "source-lighting"—which requires that light in a scene emanate from the direction of whatever source would normally provide it in real life. He also makes it standard practice to take part in the pre-production planning process for each film—reading the script, talking to the director, taking notes and telling the director what his basic approach to giving the film its more naturalistic look should be. Howe is opposed to using a technical effect simply for its own sake, as a gimmick to display one's ingenuity. He thinks that zooms are over-used today, calling them the "lazy man's tracking shot," but he is not averse to employing such techniques to increase a film's dramatic appeal. Howe is also a technician and inventor, having adapted himself to new developments in the industry and having created a counter which accurately determines the number of feet of film exposed.

Howe believes that the camera must do the cutting in a picture. He insists that a cameraman, if he is worth his salt, must know something about editing to help

THE BRAVE BULLS (1951). With Mel Ferrer. Photographed by James Wong Howe

his director. He feels that men like Howard Hawks, Victor Fleming and George Stevens cut with their cameras, shooting only what they need, unlike the newer directors who tend to overshoot. This general principle also applies to Howe's approach to lighting—he doesn't like to overlight either, because usually too much light makes for what he describes as an "unnatural" scene.

A good cameraman must also have a feel for the drama of the film, as part of his co-operation with the director. Howe believes that the basic approach of simplicity and truthfulness is the best one, and that a good cameraman gets to know and understand his techniques so well that he can mold a film any way he wants. Howe aims to achieve an unawareness by the audience of camera and lighting. Another of his rules of thumb is never to photograph what can be implied—to try to excite an audience's imagination by what it often doesn't see on screen.

Photographically, Howe's strong point has always been his adaptability—he adopts a photographic style individually crafted to draw out the specific story and characterizations. However, Howe feels that the computerized processing of today's films has taken away much of the cameraman's individuality. Regarding the difference between shooting in black and white and in color, Howe still prefers the former, although he feels that it's harder to work in black and white for the simple reason that the images in black-and-white do not tend to separate as readily as in color. Howe objects to the exaggeration of color-consciousness in many of today's films. He does not feel that color should be forced into scenes in which it does not belong, and his low-key color of The Molly Maguires is certainly every bit as effective as black-and-white technique would be.

During the many years in which Howe has been photographing Hollywood films, he has held to one constant: to interpret the subject matter photographically on the screen without disturbing its equilibrium. He gives each story feeling and meaning through his photography, yet an audience's distraction in marveling at beautiful shots offends his sense of discipline. He is most happy when his directors forget the camera and work with the people. Howe has a tendency to underplay his camera work, backed up as it is by his extraordinary technical expertise and his uncanny sense of dramatic values.

On the subject of the recent trend toward cameramen becoming directors, Howe seems content to have made two films which received decent reviews. He has often commented: "You can make directors overnight, but it takes years and years to become a cameraman." In the case of James Wong Howe, this could hardly be disputed.

Spencer Tracy in THE OLD MAN AND THE SEA (1958). Photographed by James Wong Howe

GREGORY LA CAVA

By Stephen Harvey

Now that a more knowing generation of film enthusiasts has spurned the more banal pastime of star worship for the sober vocation of directors' cults, the work of most major American filmmakers has been exhumed and dissected almost to the point of lunacy, and certainly with ever diminishing returns. Such departed masters as John Ford, Ernst Lubitsch and Preston Sturges have been lionized with the sort of prose once cornered by Hedy Lamarr's press agent, while durable contemporaries like Frank Capra and William Wellman now spend nearly as much time reliving their careers on late-night TV talk-fests as they ever did plying their craft on the sound stage three decades ago.

At the same time, this massive reassessment of an era in film history has left some surprising gaps in its wake; certainly one of the most curious has been the neglect of Gregory La Cava, whose once considerable reputation has practically evaporated since his death in 1952. At his peak, spanning roughly from 1935 to the start of World War II, La Cava was lauded by colleagues and critics for his unfaltering skill with actors and his seemingly contradictory gift for freewheeling farce and psychological insight. Nor were his films just esoteric prestige successes; most of his best films were also lucrative. Yet out of all his considerable body of work, only *Stage Door* and *My Man Godfrey* are revived with any frequency, and these are treated rather like freak successes amidst a career presumed to have been as mediocre as it now is obscure.

Yet La Cava's best work has a sophistication and emotional resonance which few of his contemporaries equaled; even a minor item such as *Bed of Roses* (1933) is surprisingly subtle and incisive in what is on the surface a standard Constance Bennett sob-story. In fact, if anything did La Cava in as far as Hollywood was concerned, it was his intransigent originality. Thanks largely to his refusal to compromise his highly individual approach to moviemaking, he was permitted to make only one film during the last ten years of his life.

Like most of the pioneers who entered the film industry during the silent era, La Cava found himself in movies more through chance than forethought. Born in a small town in Pennsylvania in 1892, La Cava initially planned to become a serious painter, but settled for working as a newspaper cartoonist in order to make a living. Logically

enough, his initiation into filmmaking came about through animation, when he accepted a stint as the chief of William Randolph Hearst Enterprises around 1917. Four years later La Cava shifted to live-action films as scenarist and then director of two-reel comedies featuring leading man Johnny Hines. Before long he had graduated to a series of independently produced Chic Sale features, and by 1925 he was ensconced at Paramount's New York studios while helming a string of popular comedies for clean-cut Richard Dix. It was during this period that he first encountered W. C. Fields, whom he directed in *So's Your Old Man* in 1926 and *Running Wild* in 1927. La Cava's pugnacious temperament and fondness for alcohol found an equal in Fields, and they remained close friends until the comedian's death in 1945.

By now established as one of the company's most promising younger directors, La Cava transferred to the more dynamic milieu of Paramount's West Coast studios in 1927. After directing ten pictures in four years at the studio, in 1929 he shifted to First National Pictures, where he simultaneously achieved his biggest success to date and began to demonstrate the kind of iconoclastic behavior that eventually made La Cava persona non grata at every studio in Hollywood. The film was a part-talkie Corinne Griffith vehicle entitled *Saturday's Children*, based on Maxwell Anderson's prestigious Broadway play. His dispute with his superiors focused on his refusal to permit anyone to supervise or tamper with his work, considered heresy in the days when the studios and their anointed moguls proclaimed the divine right to control each film they produced.

Despite La Cava's truculence, he was hired by Pathé after his swift departure from First National, and there he remained even after the studio was absorbed by RKO-Radio in 1931. La Cava's growing reputation was enhanced by such efforts as *The Half-Naked Truth* (1932), a cynical comedy about the press agent racket, closely attuned to the jaded mood of the times and to its star Lee Tracy's hard-boiled style, and *Symphony of Six Million* (1932), a persuasive Fannie Hurst tearjerker featuring Ricardo Cortez as a rising Jewish doctor and Irene Dunne as his tenement heartthrob. In 1933 La Cava signed a contract with Darryl Zanuck's Twentieth-Century Pictures (not yet merged with Fox Studios) and the fireworks erupted all over again. While shooting *Gallant*

On the set of WHAT EVERY WOMAN KNOWS (1934), with (left to right) Lucile Watson, David Torrence, Madge Evans, Dudley Digges, director Gregory La Cava (seated), Brian Aherne, Helen Hayes, and Donald Crisp

MY MAN GODFREY (1936). With Gail Patrick, Alice Brady, Carole Lombard, and William Powell

Lady (1934), one of Ann Harding's aptly named paeans to the cause of genteel martyrdom, La Cava decided that the assigned script was a hopeless botch and proceeded to shoot more or less from scratch on the set. Zanuck turned apoplectic and the conflict raged between him and La Cava until the producer relented, looked at the rushes and admitted that La Cava had saved an unlikely project.

It was at this point that the director decided to prevent a repetition of these fracases once and for all. Refusing a lucrative offer to become a contract director at MGM, La Cava became one of the few major directors with the temerity to free-lance under non-exclusive contract. Considering that the studios usually found it easier and cheaper to rely on their house roster of directors, this move entailed great risk on La Cava's part. Yet the results emphatically bore out his instincts, and this phase marked the beginning of the director's most fruitful period. During the next few years he produced a remarkably varied and interesting array of films, including *What Every Woman Knows* (1934), the J. M. Barrie standby with Helen Hayes repeating her famous stage role, *She Married Her Boss* (1935), an unusually dark Claudette Colbert comedy, *Private Worlds* (1935), a pioneering study of life inside a mental institution, and the landmark William Powell-Carole Lombard screwball farce, *My Man Godfrey* (1936). The following year La Cava won

the New York Film Critics' Circle Award for his luminous screen version of *Stage Door*, which most critics conceded to be superior to the George S. Kaufman-Edna Ferber play it was based on.

By 1940 he was garnering more than $100,000 per picture, and the contracts he elicited from his studio employers ran to over sixty pages in order to guarantee him the working freedom he demanded. By this point, too, La Cava's reputation within the industry for arrogant independence was a matter of public knowledge. An interview with the director published in *The New York Daily News* in 1940 reported that "Gregory La Cava is Hollywood's most famous no-man. He says no to every offer to make a picture unless he is sold on the story. He says no to any economy which would mar the quality of the production. He says no to every proposition to direct players who are difficult to handle and who make him unhappy with his work." Apparently nobody enjoyed perpetuating this notion of La Cava as Hollywood's *bête noire* as much as La Cava himself. The following year, *Current Biography*'s La Cava career article reinforced the image by proclaiming, "Gregory La Cava likes to think of himself as Hollywood's Neanderthal man, a rebel, a throwback, a rugged individualist, a gay sprite and a rugged non-conformist."

Naturally, this sort of breathless publicity only served to further irritate Hollywood's chiefs of state, who felt

164

that La Cava's outspoken defiance of authority was bad enough while kept pretty much a trade secret, but well-nigh intolerable when outsiders were so gleefully informed that he was getting away with it. Studio executives had long brayed that, apart from La Cava's uppity attitude, his methods were inefficient and spendthrift. As long as his films remained moneymakers, the studios found it to their interest to indulge La Cava temporarily. Yet there was little doubt that these pride-wounded giants were spoiling to give La Cava his comeuppance at the earliest opportunity.

The chance came in 1942, when *Lady in a Jam*, La Cava's million-dollar-budgeted Irene Dunne comedy, proved an unexpected fiasco with both critics and public. Obviously, every other director of such stature had been permitted to weather this sort of career crisis before and proceed to other projects, but this luxury was denied La Cava. Thanks to this one major flop and his insistence on the same freewheeling conditions he had always enjoyed, La Cava was not able to find work in Hollywood for five years. Finally in 1947 he was contracted by MGM to direct *Living in a Big Way*, a musical showcasing Gene Kelly in his first film after his discharge from the service, and Marie "The Body" McDonald, whom

certain Metro executives briefly considered major star material. The result was undistinguished, but at least it seemed to have ended the industry lockout on La Cava.

Soon thereafter he was hired by Mary Pickford's production company to write and direct the screen adaptation of Kurt Weill's musical, *One Touch of Venus*. This ill-fated venture had been on Miss Pickford's schedule for nearly five years, with Jeanette MacDonald, Ginger Rogers, Hedy Lamarr and Deanna Durbin mentioned at various times to play the mythological statue brought to life by a kiss. This time trouble flared when La Cava's propensity for shooting from a rudimentary outline drew immediate fire from Miss Pickford, who demanded a copy of the completed script to show to the financiers. Reminding Miss Pickford that he had been verbally promised complete autonomy over his work, La Cava walked off the set after eleven days of work. Soon thereafter he brought a breach of contract suit for over a million dollars against Miss Pickford; however, the case speedily went against him when his adversary pointed out that despite his claims, their written contract stipulated that Miss Pickford indeed held the right to supervise the production. This disillusioning setback spelled the finish of La Cava's directorial career; his four remaining years

Gregory La Cava on the set of STAGE DOOR (1937) with Ginger Rogers and Katharine Hepburn

FIFTH AVENUE GIRL (1939). With Ginger Rogers and Tim Holt

of life were marked by complete professional inactivity. As for the jinx-ridden *One Touch of Venus*, the final version, directed by William A. Seiter with Ava Gardner as Venus, met with a universally tepid response.

From the vantage point of today's less regimented system of moviemaking, it is hard to understand what it was about La Cava's directorial approach that so alienated the industry bosses. Yet even at present La Cava's methods would be considered somewhat unorthodox, if hardly the radical departure they seemed thirty years ago. For one thing, La Cava preferred to shoot his films more or less in sequence, rather than relying on the usual and more economical means of filming all scenes together which used the same locations. Even more controversial was La Cava's vehement refusal to abide by tightly constructed shooting scripts once filming began. Believing that no scenario polished beforehand could take account of the individual personalities and daily shifts of mood of the actors involved, La Cava chose to arrive on the set armed only with a rough outline of the day's scenes, to be fleshed out on the spot with his writers and cast. He contended that this innovation brought an

impromptu freshness and spontaneity absent in more conventionally conceived projects.

Under La Cava's guidance, an unexpected note of reality often crept into the proceedings. Thus Katharine Hepburn's skitterish comportment in the rehearsal sequence of *Stage Door* mirrored her own forthright behavior while preparing the film itself. Likewise Irene Dunne's on-screen vacillation between Robert Montgomery and Preston Foster in *Unfinished Business* probably seemed more plausible than the usual Hollywood triangular conflict because none of the actors knew exactly what the film's outcome was to be until it was completed. The performers in La Cava's films generally appreciated this system; his round-table discussions to shape theme and characterization seemed both creative and more democratic than the authoritarian measures used by many other directors. Yet such nonchalant La Cavaesque asides as his claim that "the first days, we fool around the set, just pushing the dog around" tended to induce thrombosis in the most tranquil of studio executives.

Actually, La Cava's approach wasn't that much more expensive or time-consuming than more customary meth-

166

ods. In effect, the extensive hours spent in preparation were recovered during the shooting schedule itself, as by that point La Cava was so certain of the desired effect that numerous retakes were usually unnecessary. More to the point, his technique brought demonstrable results. La Cava often stated that as a film director he was most engaged by the exploration of human emotions and psychology, rather than elaborate plots or controversial political issues. Moreover, for a man with his background in the pictorial arts, La Cava's visual style is remarkably straightforward and unadorned, in order not to detract from the interaction of character that is the keynote of his films. At his best, when aided by congenial subject matter and inventive actors, La Cava created characters whose actions and motives were both complex and strikingly naturalistic compared to the one-dimensional cartoons that have often passed for characterization in movies. Time and again La Cava proved that people in movies didn't have to be unblemished saints for audiences to sympathize with them. Assuming that the public would carry with them a certain amount of advance goodwill for stars like Claudette Colbert, Irene Dunne and the like, La Cava's gift was to inject the parts they played with a human streak of offbeat perversity.

This particular talent is evident even in the relatively early *Bed of Roses*. By this point Constance Bennett was an old hand at playing young ladies of soiled but redeemable virtue, but this time she really had her work cut out for her. This creature amuses herself for most of the picture by rolling drunks, stealing barge captain Joel McCrea's hard-earned bankroll, and blackmailing an inebriated roué into keeping her in payment for a seduction that never took place. The remarkable thing is that all these sordid details, tempered by Bennett's wry wit and La Cava's unerring subtlety, give this character a genuine human quality. Even the inevitable sudsy reunion between McCrea and Bennett can't completely undermine the impact of the four or five reels that have preceded it.

With more distinctive material to work with, as in *Private Worlds*, La Cava has the chance to throw some really startling psychological curves. This film's theme of the struggle between modern psychiatric practices and mental illness has lost its novelty thanks to *The Snake Pit*, *The Cobweb* and many other successors; what remains unusual is La Cava's exploration of the ambiguous line that divides sanity and derangement, and his compassion for those who inhabit both sides of the divide. Capable woman doctor Claudette Colbert is emotionally arrested by her romantic attachment to a suitor long since dead, colleague Joel McCrea is sporadically prone to scathing outbursts of temper, and his insecure bride Joan Bennett sees her uncertainties and sorrows reflected in

PRIMROSE PATH (1940). With Ginger Rogers and Joel McCrea

a catatonic adolescent inmate of the institution. Never do these figures descend to the level of the doctors-are-sicker-than-the-patients cliché that could easily have sabotaged the quality of the film. Instead La Cava persuasively implies that only those who have surmounted emotional problems of their own can adequately comprehend the troubled minds of others less resilient.

With the shift from the somber melodrama of *Private Worlds* to the driven merriment of *My Man Godfrey*, La Cava indulges his penchant for human idiosyncrasy nearly to the rupturing point. Although presented purely for laughs, the family Bullock is a coven of horrors worthy of Edward Albee at his most gothic. Father is a gross and insensitive boor, mother an egocentric poseuse and the eldest daughter is a smoldering shrike. The most sympathetic of this unappetizing ménage is younger daughter Carole Lombard, and to call her scatterbrained would require the unfounded assumption that she ever had any gray matter to dispose of. Under La Cava's relentless guidance their antics are hilarious, but the laughter they provoke has a slightly hollow ring to it. La Cava's real forte was the unforced intermingling of humor and pathos found in such films as *Stage Door* and *Unfinished Business*. With the balance tipped too far over

UNFINISHED BUSINESS (1941). With Irene Dunne and Robert Montgomery

into lunatic farce, the egocentrics in *My Man Godfrey* lose the tempering qualities that would have made them human as well as droll. Despite this, however, *My Man Godfrey* was one of La Cava's greatest triumphs both critically and financially, and he acknowledged this success by repeating the formula three years later in *Fifth Avenue Girl*, with Ginger Rogers substituting for William Powell as family savior.

Naturally La Cava's skill at characterization could only be as acute as the performers chosen to bring these figures to life, and he was usually quite fortunate in regard to the caliber of actors at his disposal. Stars such as Ginger Rogers, Carole Lombard, Robert Montgomery and the like were adroit professionals who rarely delivered less than amiable performances. La Cava's specialty when confronted with such personalities consisted of utilizing those aspects of their established star images that he found useful while uncovering other facets that had previously been ignored. Thus a spunky proletarian like Ginger Rogers revealed a core of genuine poignancy in *Stage Door* and particularly *Primrose Path*, in which she was cast as a gawky adolescent trapped by poverty in a mean Cannery Row shanty town. Katharine Hepburn's frosty patrician air was beginning to pall on moviegoers by 1937, so La Cava humanized her by thrusting her into the plebeian milieu of the theatrical boardinghouse of *Stage Door*. Similarly, Irene Dunne was clearly well past the ingenue stage by the time of her second outing with La Cava in 1941; however, her obvious maturity was perfectly suited to her role in *Unfinished Business*, as the perennial elder sister who escapes incipient spinsterhood by striking out on her own in the big city.

It's no accident that the most notable performances in La Cava's films were usually female. In film after film he demonstrated a singular affinity for strong and unusual women characters, and his attitudes toward them were unusually advanced for the period. La Cava heroines were never just charming and engaging; they usually displayed considerably more sense than their male opposites—*My Man Godfrey* being the one principal exception. La Cava heroes ranged the narrow gamut from ineffectual misogynists (Melvyn Douglas in *She Married Her Boss*) through self-righteous prigs (always Joel McCrea's specialty) to spineless hedonists (Robert Montgomery in *Unfinished Business*). In each case a capable woman comes along to jolt them out of their delusions of competence and lead them into accepting adult responsibilities. Along the way, La Cava heroines learn some valuable (and slightly heretical) lessons. Claudette Colbert of *Private Worlds* discovers that romance can complement her successful medical career without necessarily supplanting it, while Irene Dunne persuasively argues that women are as entitled to their share of ro-

Gene Kelly leaps fifty feet off the ground in Gregory La Cava's last film, LIVING IN A BIG WAY (1947).

mantic "unfinished business" as men are to their various pre-marital exploits.

Thus it comes as no surprise that La Cava's most thoroughly satisfying film, *Stage Door*, finds the male half of the species to be practically invisible and well-nigh irrelevant. From a historical point of view, *Stage Door* is significant as one of the most feminist films ever made in Hollywood, with its affectionate view of a wide variety of women whose lives are linked by their mutually shared career aspirations. These women belong neither to a saccharine sorority, or a bitchy viper's nest à la *The Women*, but a complex emotional community somewhere in between. Thanks to La Cava's perceptive nuances and an extraordinary array of young actresses at the outset of their careers, one has the uneasy but entirely pleasurable sensation of really witnessing the lives of these boardinghouse denizens, rather than merely an adroit impersonation thereof.

As presented on Broadway, *Stage Door* had been saddled with a few wooden romantic subplots involving the main character, plus some gratuitous, snide comparisons between the supposedly unsullied traditions of the theatre versus venal, corrupt Hollywood. La Cava, guided by Morrie Ryskind's and Anthony Veiller's superior screenplay, stripped away all this extraneous material for the film version, and the result is a nearly matchless blend of wit and pathos. Throughout, the film has an aura of effortless improvisation which actually could only have been achieved through tireless work and preparation. Caustic exchanges between Eve Arden and Lucille Ball segue without pause into poignant vignettes with doomed ingenue Andrea Leeds; Ginger Rogers coos endearments to her latest beau over the telephone while in the background her housemates complain about the cuisine. One of the measures of La Cava's triumph is that he makes it all seem so easy. Rarely calling attention to himself with unnecessary cinematic pyrotechnics, La Cava unobtrusively makes his presence felt only as an invisible intelligence shaping the material into a compelling whole. Even the undeniable moments of hokum—Hepburn's overnight sensation as the girl with the calla lilies, Andrea Leeds' suicide—are transformed into genuinely moving drama by the conviction with which they are acted and directed.

Stage Door alone should have confirmed La Cava's position as a director of unusual talent and imagination; the rest of his work serves to reinforce it. It is unfortunate that he was so often prevented in the later part of his career from exercising his formidable gifts; perhaps now at least La Cava may be accorded the recognition he found so elusive during his tempestuous years as Hollywood's self-made martyr to non-conformity.

QUIET ON THE SET

To close the book, we offer a pictorial tribute to some of the screen's most renowned directors. Here is a portfolio of photographs of the directors hard at work at various points in their careers.

Busby Berkeley gives orders on the set of BABES ON BROADWAY, a 1940 musical starring Mickey Rooney and Judy Garland. It was his third movie for MGM.

On the set of IT HAPPENED ONE NIGHT (1934), Claudette Colbert, Clark Gable, and director Frank Capra hardly suspect that they were making a classic comedy that would win them all Academy Awards.

Director Rouben Mamoulian discusses a key scene for QUEEN CHRISTINA (1933) with Greta Garbo and John Gilbert.

On the set of his adventure film, UNION PACIFIC (1939), Cecil B. DeMille talks with his stars, Barbara Stanwyck and Joel McCrea.

The crew watches as William Wellman directs a scene between Olivia de Havilland and Montgomery Clift for the 1949 drama, THE HEIRESS, from the Broadway play and the Henry James novel, *Washington Square*.

Montgomery Clift again, this time under the direction of George Stevens, in a scene for A PLACE IN THE SUN (1951), the film version of Theodore Dreiser's *An American Tragedy*. With Clift: Shelley Winters, who won an Oscar for her performance.

Katharine Hepburn with her favorite director, George Cukor, on the set of THE PHILADELPHIA STORY (1940), from the Philip Barry play.

Vincente Minnelli gesticulates as wife Judy Garland's make-up is adjusted for a scene in the 1948 Cole Porter musical, THE PIRATE.

The year: 1953. Out of costume, John Gielgud, Greer Garson, and Deborah Kerr listen to director Joseph Mankiewicz discuss a scene for the film version of William Shakespeare's JULIUS CAESAR. Also prominent in the cast: Marlon Brando and James Mason.

Starring in TERESA (1951), her first American film, Pier Angeli receives advice from director Fred Zinnemann. She played an Italian war bride who encounters prejudice in America.

Veteran director John Ford sets up a scene with John Wayne and William Holden in the 1959 Western drama, THE HORSE SOLDIERS.

In her 1949 movie, FLAMINGO ROAD, carnival girl Joan Crawford discusses a scene with director Michael Curtiz, the volatile Hungarian noted for his fractured English.

Joan Bennett takes instructions from director Fritz Lang for the 1945 melodrama, SCARLET STREET. The year before, he directed her in another melodrama THE WOMAN IN THE WINDOW, with the same co-stars, Edward G. Robinson and Dan Duryea.

Versatile director Elia Kazan also wrote and produced the 1963 film, AMERICA AMERICA. Here he talks over a scene with Stathis Giallelis, who plays a young Greek immigrant in the late 1890s.

In 1961, George Seaton directs William Holden and Lilli Palmer in THE COUNTERFEIT TRAITOR, relating the perilous adventures of a double agent.

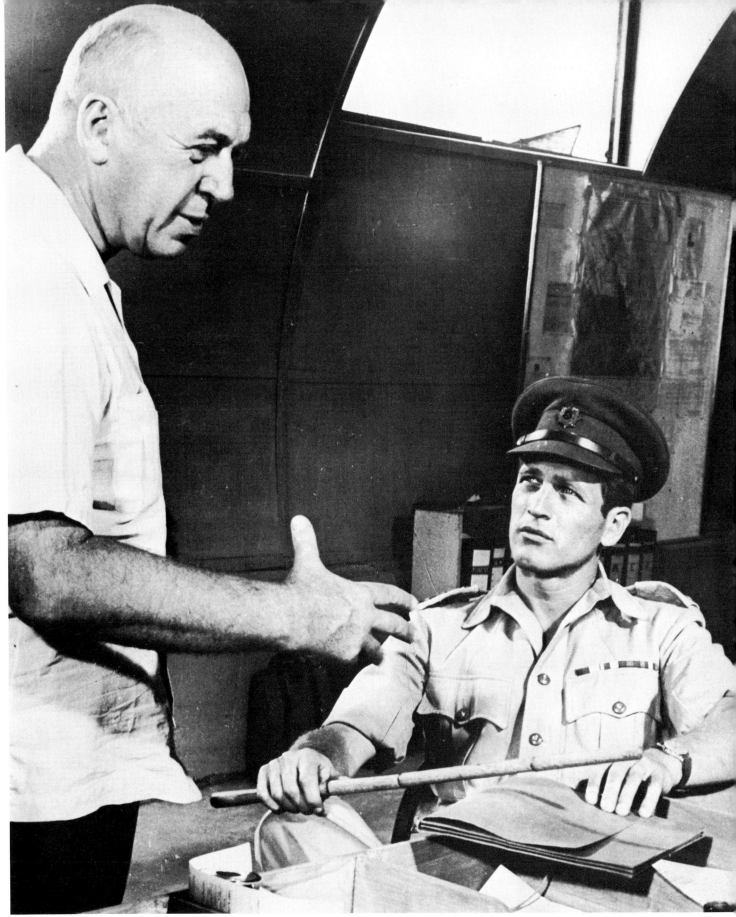

Otto Preminger directs Paul Newman in a scene for EXODUS (1960), based on Leon Uris' best-selling novel about the conflict during Israel's first years.

A cheerful pause on the set of THE APARTMENT (1960) with director Billy Wilder and star Shirley MacLaine. This witty, stinging comedy won the Academy Award for Best Picture.

ANSWERS TO QUIZZES

WHO'S THAT AGAIN?
(page 24)

1. Audrey Hepburn in *Roman Holiday* (1953)
2. Henry Fonda in *The Farmer Takes a Wife* (1935)
3. Lauren Bacall in *To Have and Have Not* (1944)
4. Deanna Durbin in *Three Smart Girls* (1937)
5. Gene Kelly in *For Me and My Gal* (1942)
6. Anna Sten in *Nana* (1934)
7. John Garfield in *Four Daughters* (1938)
8. Fred Astaire in *Dancing Lady* (1933)
9. Mario Lanza in *That Midnight Kiss* (1949)
10. Paul Newman in *The Silver Chalice* (1954)
11. Marlon Brando in *The Men* (1950)
12. James Dean in *East of Eden* (1955)
13. Jeanette MacDonald in *The Love Parade* (1929)
14. Claudette Colbert in *For the Love of Mike* (1927)
15. Tallulah Bankhead in *Tarnished Lady* (1931)

FAMILY ALBUMS—HOLLYWOOD STYLE
(page 25)

1. *The Bachelor and the Bobby-Soxer* (1947)
2. *Strange Interlude* (1932)
3. *They All Kissed the Bride* (1942)
4. *The Big Broadcast of 1938* (1938)
5. *Toys in the Attic* (1963)
6. *Undercurrent* (1947)   Also *Sylvia Scarlett* (1936)
7. *The Mountain* (1956)
8. *Conquest* (1937)
9. *That's My Boy* (1951)
10. *Riffraff* (1935)
11. *Hearts Divided* (1936)
12. *A Date With Judy* (1948)
13. *Rich, Young and Pretty* (1951)
14. *The Mortal Storm* (1940)
15. *Kings Row* (1942)
16. *Blue Hawaii* (1961)
17. *There's No Business Like Show Business* (1953)
18. *The Brothers Karamazov* (1958)
19. *Escape* (1940)
20. *Dead End* (1937)
21. *Stage Fright* (1950)
22. *Four Sons* (1940)
23. *Come Blow Your Horn* (1963)
24. *Ziegfeld Girl* (1941)
25. *Broadway Melody of 1938* (1937)

THE MOVIE CONNECTION
(page 26)

1. Both actresses played mother to the late Brandon de Wilde, Angela Lansbury in *All Fall Down* (1962) and Jean Arthur in *Shane* (1953).

2. Mary Astor and Grace Kelly both played the young wife who has an affair with Clark Gable in the African jungle, in *Red Dust* (1932, Astor) and *Mogambo* (1953, Kelly).

3. Both actors have portrayed the Devil: Laird Cregar as the suave His Excellency in *Heaven Can Wait* (1943) and Walter Huston as the sly Mr. Scratch in *All That Money Can Buy* (1941).

4. Veronica Lake was a comely sorceress in *I Married a Witch* (1942). Kim Novak was a lovely witch in *Bell, Book and Candle* (1958).

5. Maurice Chevalier played a dual role of a baron and an entertainer in the 1935 musical, *Folies Bergère*. Don Ameche starred in the 1941 remake, *That Night in Rio*, and Danny Kaye appeared in the 1951 version, *On the Riviera*.

6. In 1942 Ginger Rogers starred in *The Major and the Minor* as a young woman who impersonates a twelve-year-old in order to pay half-fare on the train. For the remake in 1955, *You're Never Too Young*, the role was changed to that of a young man, and Jerry Lewis played the part.

7. Hapless Doris Day was frightened and tormented by both actors playing scoundrelly husbands: Rex Harrison in *Midnight Lace* (1960) and Louis Jourdan in *Julie* (1956).

8. Leslie Howard and Laurence Harvey have both played Romeo in films, Howard in the 1936 version and Laurence Harvey in the 1954 version of *Romeo and Juliet*. They also played hero Philip Carey in W. Somerset Maugham's *Of Human Bondage*, Howard in 1934 and Harvey in 1964.

9. Dorothy McGuire was a put-upon mute in *The Spiral Staircase* (1946). Jane Wyman was also a hapless mute in *Johnny Belinda* (1948).

10. Both actresses have played well-known opera singers: Kathryn Grayson as Grace Moore in *So This is Love* (1953) and Eleanor Parker as Marjorie Lawrence in *Interrupted Melody* (1955).

11. All three actresses have played Queen Catherine of Russia: Bergner in *Catherine the Great* (1934), Bankhead in *A Royal Scandal* (1945) and Davis in *John Paul Jones* (1959).

12. Both players expired in the presence of Bette Davis. In *The Little Foxes* (1941), Herbert Marshall dies of a heart attack when predatory wife Davis refuses to bring him his medicine. In *Now, Voyager* (1942), Gladys Cooper dies of a heart attack when transformed daughter Davis finally tells her the blunt truth about their relationship.

13. Van Heflin and Charlton Heston have played presidents of the United States: Heflin as Andrew Johnson in *Tennessee Johnson* (1943) and Heston as Andrew Jackson in *The President's Lady* (1953).

14. Both ladies played Western sharpshooter Annie Oakley: Betty Hutton in *Annie Get Your Gun* (1950) and Barbara Stanwyck in *Annie Oakley* (1935).

15. Both actresses have appeared as young mulatto girls trying to pass for white, Susan Kohner in *Imitation of Life* (1955) and Jeanne Crain in *Pinky* (1949).

16. Both actresses have been involved on the screen in romantic liaisons with Napoleon Bonaparte: Greta Garbo in *Conquest* (1937) and Simmons in *Désirée* (1954).

17. Siobhan McKenna played Mary, Mother of Jesus, in *King of Kings* (1961). Dorothy McGuire played the same role in *The Greatest Story Ever Told* (1965).

18. Alla Nazimova was a controversial Salome in the 1923 film version of the Oscar Wilde play. Rita Hayworth was a tamer, Hollywoodized Salome in the 1953 film of the same

name. (Quick query: in which movie did the actresses appear together?) Answer below.*
19. Both Jean Arthur and Doris Day have played Western heroine Calamity Jane: Arthur in *The Plainsman* (1936) and Day in *Calamity Jane* (1953).
20. All these ladies have portrayed Mickey Rooney's mother: Fay Bainter in *Young Tom Edison* (1940) and *The Human Comedy* (1943); Fay Holden in the Hardy family films; Spring Byington in *A Family Affair* (1937, as Mrs. Hardy), and Ann Shoemaker in *Strike Up the Band* (1940).

Answer to bonus question: Both actresses have played the wife of "Dr." Paul Muni, Hutchinson in *The Story of Louis Pasteur* (1936), and Pollock in *The Last Angry Man* (1959).

* *Blood and Sand* (1941)

THE NAME GAME
(*page 38*)

1. Veronica Lake 2. Fredric March 3. Jean Arthur 4. Piper Laurie 5. Jane Wyman 6. John Wayne 7. Stewart Granger 8. Barbara Stanwyck 9. Edward Arnold 10. Boris Karloff 11. Lizabeth Scott 12. Robert Taylor 13. Jack Oakie 14. Rock Hudson 15. Shelley Winters 16. Mary Astor 17. Judy Garland 18. Edward G. Robinson 19. Claudette Colbert 20. Susan Hayward 21. Marjorie Main 22. Cyd Charisse 23. Tony Curtis 24. Ray Milland 25. Ed Wynn

THE VERSATILE PLAYERS
(*page 39*)

1. BETTY FIELD: *Of Mice and Men* (1940). *Kings Row* (1942). *The Southerner* (1945). *The Great Gatsby* (1949). *Picnic* (1955).
2. ARTHUR KENNEDY: *City for Conquest* (1940). *Devotion* (1946). *The Glass Menagerie* (1950), *Peyton Place* (1957). Hemingway's *Adventures of a Young Man* (1962).
3. THOMAS MITCHELL: *Lost Horizon* (1937). *Mr. Smith Goes to Washington* (1939). *Only Angels Have Wings* (1939). *Our Town* (1940). *A Pocketful of Miracles* (1961).
4. CLAIRE TREVOR: *Dead End* (1937). *The Desperadoes* (1943). *Key Largo* (1948). *Hard, Fast and Beautiful* (1951). *Marjorie Morningstar* (1958). *Two Weeks in Another Town* (1962).
5. CHARLES BICKFORD: *Anna Christie* (1930). *The Song of Bernadette* (1943). *Duel in the Sun* (1946). *Johnny Belinda* (1948). *A Star is Born* (1954).
6. ELSA LANCHESTER: *The Bride of Frankenstein* (1935). *Ladies in Retirement* (1941). *The Big Clock* (1948). *Witness for the Prosecution* (1958). *Bell, Book, and Candle* (1958).
7. MARY ASTOR: *Don Juan* (1926). *The Palm Beach Story* (1942). *Meet Me in St. Louis* (1944). *Act of Violence* (1948). *Return to Peyton Place* (1961).
8. BURGESS MEREDITH: *Winterset* (1936). *Of Mice and Men* (1939). *That Uncertain Feeling* (1941). *Tom, Dick and Harry* (1941). *The Story of GI Joe* (1945).
9. ADOLPHE MENJOU: *Gold Diggers of 1935* (1935). *Stage Door* (1937). *Golden Boy* (1940). *A Bill of Divorcement* (1940). *State of the Union* (1948).

10. J. CARROL NAISH: *Sahara* (1943). *A Medal for Benny* (1945). *Humoresque* (1946). *The Black Hand* (1950). *Annie Get Your Gun* (1950).
11. AGNES MOOREHEAD: *The Magnificent Ambersons* (1942). *Since You Went Away* (1944). *Dark Passage* (1947). *Show Boat* (1951). *The Opposite Sex* (1956). *Hush . . . Hush, Sweet Charlotte* (1964).
12. WALTER HUSTON: *Rain* (1932). *Dodsworth* (1936). *All That Money Can Buy* (1941). *Edge of Darkness* (1943). *The Treasure of the Sierra Madre* (1948).
13. LOUIS CALHERN: *Duck Soup* (1933). *Annie Get Your Gun* (1950). *The Asphalt Jungle* (1950). *The Magnificent Yankee* (1951). *Julius Caesar* (1953).
14. MIRIAM HOPKINS: *Trouble in Paradise* (1932). *She Loves Me Not* (1934). *These Three* (1936). *Old Acquaintance* (1943). *Carrie* (1952).
Extra Question:
BEULAH BONDI: *Make Way for Tomorrow* (1937). *Mr. Smith Goes to Washington* (1939). *Penny Serenade* (1941). *Watch on the Rhine* (1943). *The Track of the Cat* (1954).

THE GOLDEN SILENCE
(*page 40*)

1. Douglas Fairbanks, *The Thief of Bagdad* (1924)
2. ZaSu Pitts, *Greed* (1924)
3. Janet Gaynor, *Seventh Heaven* (1927)
4. Erich Von Stroheim, *Foolish Wives* (1922)
5. Mary Pickford, *Tess of the Storm Country* (1914, also 1922)
6. Richard Barthelmess, *Broken Blossoms* (1919)
7. John Barrymore, *Beau Brummel* (1924)
8. Dorothy Gish, *Hearts of the World* (1918)
9. Greta Garbo, *Flesh and the Devil* (1927)
10. Lon Chaney, *He Who Gets Slapped* (1924)
11. Joan Crawford, *Our Dancing Daughters* (1928)
12. George Arliss, *The Man Who Played God* (1922)
13. Harry Langdon, *The Strong Man* (1926)
14. Rudolph Valentino, *Blood and Sand* (1922)
15. Lillian Gish, *The White Sister* (1923)
16. Charlie Chaplin, *The Circus* (1928)
17. Buster Keaton, *Sherlock, Jr.* (1924)
18. Harold Lloyd, *Safety Last* (1923)
19. Gloria Swanson, *Male and Female* (1919)
20. Renée Adorée, *The Big Parade* (1926)

PROFESSIONALLY SPEAKING
(*page 41*)

Doctors
1. Joel McCrea.
2. *Not As a Stranger* and *The Cobweb* (both 1955).
3. Clark Gable in *Men in White*.
4. Margaret Sullavan in *Appointment For Love* (1941), Barbara Stanwyck in *You Belong to Me* (1941), June Allyson in *The Girl in White* (1952), Ingrid Bergman in *Spellbound* (1945), Greer Garson in *Strange Lady in Town* (1955), Aline MacMahon in *The Young Doctors* (1961), and doubtlessly others.
5. *Crisis*.

Lawyers
1. Arthur Kennedy.
2. *The People Against O'Hara.*
3. Adolphe Menjou.
4. *The Letter* (1940). James Stephenson
5. George C. Scott.

Teachers
1. Martha Scott, *Cheers for Miss Bishop* (1941).
2. Sidney Poitier, *To Sir, With Love* (1967).
3. Glenn Ford, *The Blackboard Jungle* (1955).
4. Claudette Colbert, *Remember the Day* (1941).
5. John Houseman, *The Paper Chase* (1973).

Nurses
1. Anna Neagle.
2. Margaret Sullavan, Joan Blondell, Ann Sothern, Fay Bainter, Ella Raines, Frances Gifford, Marsha Hunt.
3. Anne Shirley.
4. Alma Kruger.
5. Patricia Neal.

Actors
1. Ronald Colman in *A Double Life* (1947).
2. Ginger Rogers in *Forever Female* (1953).
3. Janet Gaynor and Judy Garland in *A Star Is Born* (1937 and 1954).
4. Anthony Franciosa in *Career* (1960).
5. Jean Harlow in *Bombshell* (1933).

Writers
1. Olivia de Havilland in *Devotion* (1946).
2. James Mason in *Madame Bovary* (1949).
3. Gregory Peck in *Beloved Infidel* (1959).
4. Merle Oberon in *A Song to Remember* (1945).
5. Herbert Marshall in *The Razor's Edge* (1946).

THEY HAD CHARACTER
(page 42)

Photo 1. Glenda Farrell, Ned Sparks.
Photo 2. *One Way Passage.*
Photo 3. Frank Faylen.
Photo 4. *Gentleman Jim* (as Errol Flynn's father, 1942), *They Drive By Night* (as Ida Lupino's husband, 1940).
Photo 5. Everett Sloane.
Photo 6. Walter Connolly, Lee Tracy.
Photo 7. Porter Hall.
Photo 8. Steven Geray (bartender), Joseph Calleia (crouching policeman), George Macready (corpse).
Photo 9. Don Beddoe.
Photo 10. Conrad Veidt. *A Woman's Face* (1941), *All Through the Night* (1941).
Photo 11. *Summer Storm.*
Photo 12. Wallace Ford.
Photo 13. Helen Westley.
Photo 14. Alice Brady.
Photo 15. Elizabeth Patterson.
Photo 16. Charles Butterworth.
Photo 17. Clarence Kolb
Photo 18. George Tobias (1942), Kurt Kasznar (1955).
Photo 19. Una O'Connor.
Photo 20. Mildred Dunnock.

SONGS, DANCES, AND SNAPPY SAYINGS
(page 62)

I. a. *The Harvey Girls* (1946). John Hodiak ran the Alhambra Café. Judy Garland, Cyd Charisse, and Virginia O'Brien sang "It's a Great Big World." "The Train Must Be Fed" was another song from the film.

b. *She Loves Me Not* (1934). Bing Crosby sang "Love In Bloom." Kitty Carlisle (Mrs. Moss Hart) played the romantic lead. *How to Be Very, Very Popular* was a 1955 movie largely based on *She Loves Me Not.*

c. *The Gay Divorcée* (1934). Claire Luce played opposite Astaire in the original stage version, *Gay Divorce*. "Let's K-nock K-nees" was a song rendered by Edward Everett Horton and Betty Grable. The immortal lines were delivered by Erik Rhodes as the professional corespondent, Tonetti.

d. *On the Avenue* (1937). "Let's Go Slumming" was one of the Irving Berlin songs. The Ritz Brothers appeared in the film. "The pretty young brunette" was sung about by Dick Powell in a production number.

e. *Seven Brides for Seven Brothers* (1954). "Spring, Spring, Spring" was one of the songs. Stephen Vincent Benét wrote the original story on which the film was based. Michael Kidd staged the brilliant dances.

f. *Funny Face* (1957). "He Loves and She Loves" was a lyrical number by Fred Astaire and Audrey Hepburn. "Emphaticalism" was the philosophy that book clerk Audrey Hepburn found so fascinating. Maggie Prescott was the name of Kay Thompson's character of the chic fashion magazine editor.

g. *Anchors Aweigh* (1945). The Girl from Brooklyn (identified this way throughout the film) was Frank Sinatra's girlfriend. Pamela Britton played the role. "All of a Sudden My Heart Sings" was rendered by Kathryn Grayson. Dean Stockwell played her little nephew.

h. *Cabin in the Sky* (1943). Lucifer, Jr. (Rex Ingram) headed up the public relations department of Hades. "Life's Full of Consequences" was one of the songs. Vernon Duke wrote the music of the original stage play, some of which was retained in the film version.

i. *Ziegfeld Follies* (1946). "Pay the Two Dollars" was a sketch with Victor Moore and Edward Arnold. In the musical number, "This Heart of Mine," Fred Astaire was the jewel thief, and Lucille Bremer was his victim. "Love is like a burning ember" is a line from Lena Horne's scorching song, "Love."

j. *Summer Holiday* (1948). Cousin Lily (Agnes Moorehead) was the Miller family's resident spinster. "Weary Blues" was sung by bar-girl Marilyn Maxwell to an intoxicated Mickey Rooney. The line was spoken by Walter Huston to Selena Royle at the close of the film.

II. a. *Two Girls and a Sailor* (1944)
b. *Small Town Girl* (1953)
c. *Weekend in Havana* (1941)
d. *Ready, Willing and Able* (1937)
e. *Born to Dance* (1936)
f. *Alexander's Ragtime Band* (1938)
g. *Captain January* (1936)
h. *Music for Millions* (1944)
i. *High Society* (1956)
j. *High, Wide and Handsome* (1937)

III. a. *To Have and Have Not* (1944)
b. *Dark Victory* (1939)

c. *Key Largo* (1948)
d. *Adam's Rib* (1949)
e. *Destry Rides Again* (1939)
f. *A Guy Named Joe* (1944)
g. *Moulin Rouge* (1953)
h. *The Picture of Dorian Gray* (1945)
i. *Road House* (1948)
j. *The Razor's Edge* (1946)

IV. a. *Flying Down to Rio* (1933).
b. Betty Hutton (*Let's Dance*, 1950).
c. "The Piccolino" (*Top Hat*, 1935).
d. George Burns and Gracie Allen.
e. Eric Blore was the officious waiter in *The Gay Divorcée* (1934), the supercilious valet in *Top Hat* (1935), the manager of a dance school in *Swing Time* (1936), and the hotel manager in *Shall We Dance* (1937).
f. *Roberta* (1935), Huckleberry Haines.
g. *The Story of Vernon and Irene Castle* (1939). *On the Beach* (1959).
h. *Royal Wedding* (1951).
i. *Swing Time* (1936).
j. Astaire starred in *Silk Stockings* (1957), the film version of the stage musical based on *Ninotchka* (1939), the film in which Greta Garbo starred. (No, they did *not* play the same role.)

THE ILLS THAT FLESH IS HEIR TO
(*page 65*)

1. *The Snake Pit* (1948), Olivia de Havilland.
2. *The Lost Weekend* (1945), Ray Milland.
3. *Bigger Than Life* (1956), James Mason.
4. *The Man With the Golden Arm* (1955), Frank Sinatra.
5. *The Seventh Veil* (1945), Ann Todd.
6. *The Bad Seed* (1956), Patty McCormack.
7. *Days of Wine and Roses* (1962), Lee Remick.
8. *The Lady Gambles* (1949), Barbara Stanwyck.
9. *Spellbound* (1945), Gregory Peck.
10. *Come Back, Little Sheba* (1952), Burt Lancaster.
11. *A Hatful of Rain* (1957), Don Murray.
12. *Possessed* (1947), Joan Crawford.
13. *Suddenly, Last Summer* (1959), Elizabeth Taylor.
14. *The Dark Mirror* (1946), Olivia de Havilland.
15. *I'll Cry Tomorrow* (1955), Susan Hayward.
16. *Don't Bother to Knock* (1952), Marilyn Monroe.
17. *The Mark* (1961), Stuart Whitman.
18. *Pressure Point* (1962), Bobby Darin.
19. *Rebel Without a Cause* (1955), James Dean.
20. *Fear Strikes Out* (1957), Anthony Perkins.

"AND I QUOTE . . ."
(*page 66*)

1. *Camille* (1936)
2. *The Grapes of Wrath* (1940)
3. *Dr. Strangelove* (1964)
4. *The Treasure of the Sierra Madre* (1948)
5. *Duck Soup* (1933)

6. *How Green Was My Valley* (1941)
7. *The Informer* (1935)
8. *Mutiny on the Bounty* (1935)
9. *Double Indemnity* (1944)
10. *I Am a Fugitive From a Chain Gang* (1932)
11. *Harper* (1966)
12. *Guess Who's Coming to Dinner* (1967)
13. *King Kong* (1933)
14. *The Women* (1936)
15. *The Public Enemy* (1931)
16. *Touch of Evil* (1958)
17. *Born Yesterday* (1950)
18. *My Little Chickadee* (1940)
19. *A Tree Grows in Brooklyn* (1945)
20. *All Quiet on the Western Front* (1930)
21. *You Can't Take It With You* (1938)
22. *Pat and Mike* (1952)
23. *Fury* (1936)
24. *Casablanca* (1942)
25. *She Done Him Wrong* (1933)
26. *Top Hat* (1935)
27. *For Whom the Bell Tolls* (1943)
28. *Mr. Smith Goes to Washington* (1939)
29. *Watch on the Rhine* (1943)
30. *Sunset Boulevard* (1950)
31. *The African Queen* (1951)
32. *Now, Voyager* (1942)
33. *White Heat* (1950)
34. *Funny Girl* (1968)
35. *All About Eve* (1950)
36. *It Happened One Night* (1934)
37. *The Life of Emile Zola* (1937)
38. *San Francisco* (1936)
39. *The Maltese Falcon* (1941)
40. *The Apartment* (1960)
41. *The Bridge on the River Kwai* (1957)
42. *On the Waterfront* (1954)
43. *Key Largo* (1948)
44. *Ninotchka* (1939)
45. *Rebecca* (1940)
46. *Mrs. Miniver* (1942)
47. *Monsieur Verdoux* (1964)
48. *The Good Earth* (1937)
49. *To Be or Not To Be* (1942)
50. *In Which We Serve* (1942)

THE MOVIE SCENE
(*page 68*)

Photo 1: *Morocco*
Photo 2: *The Bitter Tea of General Yen*
Photo 3: *Man's Castle*
Photo 4: *The Mask of Fu Manchu*
Photo 5: *Broadway Bill*
Photo 6: *The Awful Truth*
Photo 7: *Let's Do It Again*
Photo 8: *City for Conquest*
Photo 9: *Each Dawn I Die*
Photo 10: *Mr. and Mrs. Smith*
Photo 11: *Ziegfeld Girl* • *Love Finds Andy Hardy*

Photo 12: *The Bride of Frankenstein*
Photo 13: *Bordertown*
Photo 14: *Humoresque*
Photo 15: *It Should Happen to You*
Photo 16: *The Member of the Wedding*

17. *M* (1932) (remade in 1951)
18. *L'Avventura* (1960)
19. *The Seventh Seal* (1956)
20. *Potemkin* (1926)
21. *Mr. Hulot's Holiday* (1954)
22. *Divorce—Italian Style* (1962)
23. *Forbidden Games* (1952)
24. *8½* (1963)
25. *Shoe Shine* (1947)

DO IT AGAIN
(page 77)

The Major and the Minor
The Shop Around the Corner
Love Is News
Swing High, Swing Low
Lady For A Day
Nothing Sacred
It Happened One Night
My Favorite Wife
Tom, Dick and Harry
The Philadelphia Story
Wife, Husband and Friend
Too Many Husbands
True Confession
*The Greeks Had a Word
  For It*
It Started With Eve
Midnight
Bachelor Mother
Mad About Music
Ninotchka
Brother Rat
The Lady Eve
You Belong To Me
The More the Merrier
The Male Animal

Libeled Lady

You're Never Too Young
In the Good Old Summertime
That Wonderful Urge
When My Baby Smiles at Me
A Pocketful of Miracles
Living It Up
You Can't Run Away from It
Move Over, Darling
The Girl Most Likely
High Society
Everybody Does It
Three for the Show
Cross My Heart
How to Marry a Millionaire

I'd Rather Be Rich
Masquerade in Mexico
Bundle of Joy
The Toy Tiger
Silk Stockings
About Face
The Birds and the Bees
Emergency Wedding
Walk, Don't Run
*She's Working Her Way
  Through College*
Easy to Wed

FOREIGN MATTER
(page 83)

1. *Grand Illusion* (1937)
2. *Wild Strawberries* (1959)
3. *Rififi* (1955)
4. *Rashomon* (1951)
5. *La Dolce Vita* (1960)
6. *The Bicycle Thief* (1949)
7. *The Shop on Main Street* (1965)
8. *Paisan* (1948)
9. *The Blue Angel* (1929) (remade in 1959)
10. *The 400 Blows* (1958)
11. *Mayerling* (1937) (remade in 1968)
12. *Gate of Hell* (1954)
13. *Children of Paradise* (1945)
14. *Open City* (1946)
15. *Ikiru* (1952)
16. *La Strada* (1956)

TO THE LADIES
(page 84)

1. *All the King's Men* (1949), Mercedes McCambridge.
2. *Meet Me in St. Louis* (1944), Judy Garland.
3. *Notorious* (1946), Ingrid Bergman.
4. *Duel in the Sun* (1946), Jennifer Jones.
5. *My Man Godfrey* (1936 and 1957), Carole Lombard and June Allyson.
6. *Stage Door* (1937), Katharine Hepburn.
7. *Adam's Rib* (1949), Judy Holliday.
8. *Harvey* (1950), Josephine Hull.
9. *I Want to Live!* (1958), Susan Hayward.
10. *Stage Fright* (1950), Marlene Dietrich.
11. *The Best of Everything* (1959), Joan Crawford.
12. *Dinner At Eight* (1933), Marie Dressler.
13. *Animal Crackers* (1930), Margaret Dumont.
14. *From Here to Eternity* (1953), Deborah Kerr.
15. *Wuthering Heights* (1939), Geraldine Fitzgerald.
16. *Lady in the Dark* (1944), Ginger Rogers.
17. *The Maltese Falcon* (1941), Mary Astor.
18. *Ninotchka* (1939), Greta Garbo.
19. *A Foreign Affair* (1948), Marlene Dietrich.
20. *Ball of Fire* (1941), Barbara Stanwyck.
21. *The Awful Truth* (1937), Irene Dunne.
22. *The Heiress* (1949), Olivia de Havilland.
23. *Giant* (1956), Elizabeth Taylor.
24. *Woman of the Year* (1941), Katharine Hepburn.
25. *The Subject Was Roses* (1968), Patricia Neal.

GENTLEMEN OF THE MOVIES
(page 85)

1. *High Noon* (1952), Gary Cooper.
2. *Scarface* (1932), Paul Muni.
3. *Angels With Dirty Faces* (1938), James Cagney.
4. *Witness for the Prosecution* (1958), Charles Laughton.
5. *Dr. Strangelove* (1964), Keenan Wynn.
6. *The Pajama Game* (1957), John Raitt.
7. *The Collector* (1965), Terence Stamp.
8. *20th Century* (1934), John Barrymore.
9. *The Hustler* (1961), Paul Newman.
10. *Ruggles of Red Gap* (1935), Charlie Ruggles.
11. *Four Daughters* (1938) (also the sequels), Claude Rains.
12. *The Bad and the Beautiful* (1952), Kirk Douglas.
13. *Shadow of a Doubt* (1943), Joseph Cotten.
14. *The Sweet Smell of Success* (1957), Tony Curtis.

15. *Charade* (1963), Cary Grant.
16. *Separate Tables* (1958), David Niven.
17. *Picnic* (1955), Arthur O'Connell.
18. *Laura* (1944), Vincent Price.
19. *Kid Galahad* (1937), Edward G. Robinson.
20. *Compulsion* (1959), Orson Welles.
21. *To Kill a Mockingbird* (1962), Gregory Peck.
22. *Some Like It Hot* (1959), Joe E. Brown.
23. *The Miracle of Morgan's Creek* (1943), Eddie Bracken.
24. *The Misfits* (1961), Clark Gable.
25. *Gaslight* (1944), Charles Boyer.

MURDER AND MAYHEM

(page 86)

1. *Rope* (1948)
2. *Psycho* (1960)
3. *Ladies in Retirement* (1941)
4. *The Stranger* (1946)
5. *The Spiral Staircase* (1946)
6. *Deception* (1946)
7. *Rebecca* (1940)
8. *Crossfire* (1947)
9. *The Letter* (1940)
10. *Wait Until Dark* (1967)
11. *Sorry, Wrong Number* (1948)
12. *White Heat* (1949)
13. *Julie* (1956)
14. *Kiss of Death* (1947)
15. *Sudden Fear* (1952)
16. *The Big Clock* (1948)
17. *Sunset Boulevard* (1950)
18. *The Petrified Forest* (1936)
19. *Lady in a Cage* (1964)
20. *Bad Day at Black Rock* (1954)

DISNEY AND HIS FRIENDS

(page 90)

1. *Dumbo.*
2. Deems Taylor (narrator), Leopold Stokowski (conductor).
3. Harry Stockwell, Dean Stockwell (played child murderer in *Compulsion*).
4. *Alice in Wonderland.*
5. *Melody Time.*
6. Lampwick.
7. *The Absent-Minded Professor.*
8. Jane Darwell.
9. Kathryn Beaumont.
10. *Bambi.*
11. Hayley Mills.
12. James MacArthur.
13. Panchito.
14. John Mills.
15. *So Dear to My Heart.*
16. Jerry Colonna.
17. *The Jungle Book.*
18. Ed Wynn.
19. Flower the skunk.
20. James Mason.
21. Merriweather.
22. Marge Champion.
23. Buddy Ebsen.
24. Bing Crosby.
25. *The Living Desert.*

THEM THAR HILLS

(page 92)

1. John Carradine
2. *Convicted*
3. *Gun for a Coward*
4. *Santa Fe Trail* (1940) and *Seven Angry Men* (1955)
5. *Red River*
6. All played Western lawman Doc Holliday: Walter Huston in *The Outlaw* (1943), Victor Mature in *My Darling Clementine* (1946), and Kirk Douglas in *Gunfight at the O.K. Corral* (1957).
7. Mercedes McCambridge
8. *House of Strangers*
9. Katharine Ross
10. *The Oklahoma Kid* (1939), *Run For Cover* (1955), and *Tribute to a Bad Man* (1956) were Cagney Westerns.
11. John Wayne
12. Both played "hanging judge" Roy Bean: Walter Brennan in *The Westerner* (1940) and Paul Newman in *The Life and Times of Judge Roy Bean* (1972)
13. Anthony Quinn
14. The Cooper role was played by Joel McCrea; the Huston role by Brian Donlevy
15. Marlon Brando
16. Skip Homeier
17. *High Sierra*
18. *Dodge City* (1939), *Virginia City* (1940), *Santa Fe Trail* (1940), and *San Antonio* (1945).
19. Joanne Dru
20. Donald Meek's role was played by Red Buttons; Thomas Mitchell's role was played by Bing Crosby.

RULE, BRITANNIA!

(page 94)

1. Margaret Rutherford. *Blithe Spirit* (1945)
2. *The Happiest Days of Your Life* (1950)
3. Robert Morley. Rex Harrison
4. Binnie Barnes
5. *Stairway to Heaven* (1946)
6. Carol Reed. A mine disaster: *The Stars Look Down* (1941). An Irish fugitive: *Odd Man Out* (1947). Zither music: *The Third Man* (1950). "Where Is Love?": *Oliver!* (1968)
7. An antique car
8. *The Thirty-Nine Steps* (1935)
9. *Evergreen* (1935)
10. Margaret Leighton
11. Wilfrid Lawson

12. Michael Redgrave. Maxwell Frere: *Dead of Night* (1946). Andrew Crocker-Harris: *The Browning Version* (1951). Ernest Worthing: *The Importance of Being Earnest* (1952)
13. Joan Greenwood
14. A commuter train
15. *Encore*
16. Petula Clark
17. Gregory Peck. Mark Twain
18. *The Long Dark Hall*
19. Terence Rattigan
20. *Kind Hearts and Coronets* (1950)
21. *The Four Feathers*
22. *The Battle of the Sexes*
23. Elisabeth Bergner
24. Barry Jones
25. Audrey Hepburn

A CROSSWORD PUZZLE FOR MOVIE BUFFS
(*page 96*)

THE DIRECTOR'S CHAIR (I)
(*page 150*)

I. Alfred Hitchcock
   A. *Lifeboat* (1944)
   B. Dame May Whitty
   C. *Foreign Correspondent* (1940)
   D. *Notorious* (1946)
   E. *Saboteur* (1942)
II. John Ford
   A. *The Quiet Man* (1952)
   B. *Mary of Scotland* (1936)
   C. Russell Simpson
   D. William Powell
   E. John Wayne
III. William Wyler
   A. *The Little Foxes* (1941)
   B. *Jezebel* (1938)
   C. *The Children's Hour* (1962). The altered earlier version was *These Three* (1936).
   D. *The Best Years of Our Lives* (1946). Harold Russell
   E. *Dead End* (1937) and *The Desperate Hours* (1955)
IV. Cecil B. DeMille
   A. *The Plainsman* (1936), Jean Arthur.
   B. *Reap the Wild Wind* (1942)
   C. Emmett Kelly
   D. Boris Karloff, Walter Hampden.
   E. Claudette Colbert
V. George Cukor
   A. *The Philadelphia Story* (1940)
   B. Nobody. The character never appeared in the film.
   C. Aldo Ray
   D. *A Bill of Divorcement* (1932)
   E. Constance Bennett

THE DIRECTOR'S CHAIR (II)
(*page 151*)

1. *Magic Town*
2. *The Valley of Decision*
3. *Mr. 880*
4. *Yolanda and the Thief*
5. *Dive Bomber*
6. *The Long Night*
7. *No Way Out*
8. *Mr. Skeffington*
9. *Christmas in Connecticut*
10. *Claudia and David*
11. *My Favorite Wife*
12. *In the Good Old Summertime*
13. *The Thin Man Goes Home*
14. *Edge of Darkness*
15. *Sundown*
16. *Silk Stockings*
17. *Quartet*
18. *Come to the Stable*
19. *The Moon Is Down*
20. *The Mating Season*
21. *The Tall Men*
22. *Five Branded Women*
23. *Dodge City*
24. *To Each His Own*
25. *Curly Top*

THE MOVIE SONGSMITHS
(page 153)

"Sure Thing," Jerome Kern, *Cover Girl.*

"You Are Too Beautiful," Richard Rodgers, *Hallelujah, I'm a Bum.*

"Too Late Now," Burton Lane, *Royal Wedding.*

"A Boy Chases A Girl," Irving Berlin, *There's No Business Like Show Business.*

"Young and Healthy," Harry Warren, *42nd Street.*

"Things Are Looking Up," George Gershwin, *A Damsel in Distress.*

"You Stepped Out of a Dream," Nacio Herb Brown, *Ziegfeld Girl.*

"Honey in the Honeycomb," Harold Arlen, *Cabin in the Sky.*

"Love Thy Neighbor," Harry Revel, *We're Not Dressing.*

"This Heart of Mine," Hugh Martin, *Ziegfeld Follies.*

"I Fall in Love Too Easily," Jule Styne, *Anchors Aweigh.*

"Anywhere I Wander," Frank Loesser, *Hans Christian Andersen.*

"The Day After Forever," Jimmy Van Heusen, *Going My Way.*

"Thanks For the Memory," Ralph Rainger, *The Big Broadcast of 1938.*

"You Can Do No Wrong," Cole Porter, *The Pirate.*

"I Guess I'll Have to Change My Plan," Arthur Schwartz, *The Bandwagon.*

"It's a Most Unusual Day," Jimmy McHugh, *A Date With Judy.*

UNHERALDED AND UNSUNG
(page 154)

1b. *Goodbye, Mr. Chips*
2a. *A Place in the Sun*
3c. *Dr. Zhivago*
4a. a cinematographer who photographed *Casablanca*
5c. Joseph Stefano
6c. Frank Borzage for *Seventh Heaven*
7b. MGM's art director for many years
8c. *The Bishop's Wife*
9b. Anatole Litvak
10a. a composer of many film scores
11c. *Centennial Summer*
12b. *Solomon and Sheba*
13b. Lloyd Bacon
14a. *Donovan's Reef*
15b. W. Somerset Maugham
16b. a busy screenwriter for Warners in the thirties and forties
17c. *Easy Living*
18b. A blinded war veteran named Al Schmid tries to return to normal life, with great difficulty. (This was *Pride of the Marines*; the other films were *Stella Dallas* and *Ball of Fire*.)
19c. Marni Nixon
20a. "The Shadow of Your Smile," from *The Sandpiper*
21b. *Ivanhoe*
22c. Nunnally Johnson
23b. Daniel Mann
24c. one of the few women directors in film history
25b. Natalie Kalmus

ABOUT THE CONTRIBUTORS

Jeanine Basinger teaches film courses at Wesleyan University and has written on film for *The New York Times* and for The University of Connecticut Film Study Center. She is the author of a volume in the Pyramid Illustrated History of the Movies on Shirley Temple.

Curtis F. Brown has written a book on Ingrid Bergman for the Pyramid Illustrated History of the Movies. A film addict for many years, he is an administrative assistant at a New York college.

Gary Collins has written on film for *Scroll, Photon,* and *The Velvet Light Trap.* He holds a Master's Degree in Film from Wesleyan University.

Stephen Harvey is author of a book on Joan Crawford in the Pyramid film series. He has written for *Film Comment* and currently works in the Department of Film at the Museum of Modern Art.

Foster Hirsch has contributed two books to the Pyramid film series: *Elizabeth Taylor* and *Edward G. Robinson.* He has also written critical studies of the plays of Tennessee Williams and George Kelly. He has written on films, theatre, and books for many publications, including *The Nation, The New Republic, The New York Times, The Village Voice, Film Quarterly,* and *Film Heritage.* He is an Assistant Professor of English at Brooklyn College.

René Jordan has written books for the Pyramid film series on Clark Gable, Marlon Brando, and Gary Cooper. He is also the author of a book on Barbra Streisand. He has written extensively on films for many publications, including *Film Quarterly, The Village Voice, Films in Review, Cinema,* and *Film Ideal.*

Robert F. Moss is the author of Pyramid volumes on the horror film and Charlie Chaplin. He is an Assistant Professor of English at Rutgers University with a strong interest in film. He has published film criticism in *Film Heritage, Film Quarterly,* and *The New York Times.*

Howard Thompson has been a staff reviewer of films, plays, and television for *The New York Times* for over twenty-five years. He contributed a book on James Stewart to the Pyramid Illustrated History of the Movies and has also written a book on Fred Astaire. He edited *The New York Times Book of Movies on TV.*

Jerry Vermilye has contributed three volumes to the Pyramid film series: on Bette Davis, Cary Grant, and Barbara Stanwyck. He has also written books on Burt Lancaster and Elizabeth Taylor. An incurable movie buff, his reviews and articles have appeared in *Films in Review, Film Fan Monthly, Screen Facts, The Independent Film Journal,* and Andy Warhol's *InterView.* At present, he is movie-listings editor of *TV Guide.*

William Wolf has been film critic of *Cue* magazine since 1964. He is former chairman of the New York Film Critics, and an internationally syndicated writer. He teaches "Film as Literature" at New York University and "Contemporary Cinema" at St. John's University. He is also the author of a forthcoming book on the Marx Brothers in the Pyramid film series.

Nicholas Yanni is the author of two books in the Pyramid Illustrated History of the Movies: *W. C. Fields* and a forthcoming volume on Rosalind Russell. He has written on film for many publications and recently taught film courses at Brooklyn College.

ABOUT THE EDITOR

Ted Sennett is the author of *Warner Brothers Presents,* a tribute to the great Warners' films of the thirties and forties, and of *Lunatics and Lovers,* on the long-vanished but well-remembered "screwball" comedies of the past. He is the General Editor of the Pyramid Illustrated History of the Movies.